HOLLYWOOD looks at its audience

Hollywood looks at its audience

A report of film audience research

BY LEO A. HANDEL

THE UNIVERSITY OF ILLINOIS PRESS, URBANA : 1950

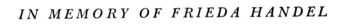

IN MEMORY OF FRIEDA HANDEL

PREFACE

This book was made possible by two men who excel in their respective fields of activity. One is Howard Dietz, vice-president of Metro-Goldwyn-Mayer, whose realistic questioning of film audience research enabled me to conduct extensive studies in this area of research. The other is Columbia University's Paul F. Lazarsfeld, whose trailblazing work in radio research inspired me to study motion picture audiences along similar lines.

It is, therefore, no coincidence that this book, which owes so much to the encouragement of a leader of the film industry and a pioneer of social research, aims to be of interest to two groups of readers. It attempts to show the student of research how the survey technique is actually used by the motion picture industry; and it takes the film executive backstage in the research office, to familiarize him with the techniques of public opinion sampling.

I wish to acknowledge gratefully the following contributions to this volume. Robert Bower, of the University of America, undertook the laborious assignment of the final editing of the book. The late Jay A. Gove, former head of Metro-Goldwyn-Mayer's sales development department, co-operated with me on the chapter dealing with the evaluative studies of the industry. Also Ruth A. Inglis, University of Washington, and Thomas W. Gerety, of Metro-Goldwyn-Mayer, frequently gave me the benefit of their advice.

LEO A. HANDEL

FOREWORD

From time to time it is worthwhile to speculate as to why the field of communications research has had such a rapid growth. Fifteen years ago the term had not yet been invented, and several years ago the area had only a bare existence. Today we have a large literature and courses are taught in numerous universities. Several research centers, notable among them the Institute of Communications Research at the University of Illinois, specialize in problems of mass communications. It is true that some of these developments spring from the commercial needs of newer branches of the communications industry. The printed media have their circulation records and the movies have their box-offices. Radio and television have to do their own research if they want to know whether they have any audience at all. It is also true that the needs of the newer media have in turn influenced the older ones. The printed media which competed with radio and television for advertising revenue needed increasingly refined data.

But there are more basic social forces behind the development of communications research, and they are closely related to the contemporary political scene. Since the end of World War II, we have witnessed the development of a new type of relationship between blocks of countries. It is not the type represented by the British Empire at the height of its power, when large colonial areas were administered by a small force of civil servants directed from London. Nor is it like the old "spheres of influence," which were based mainly on economic advantages conceded by smaller to stronger powers. We do not even have a name yet for this new development because it appears in so

many forms. The satellite countries behind the Iron Curtain
are dominated by political parties which, in turn, are directed
by the Communist Party in Russia. The countries of the Western Union in Europe are politically free, but they depend for
defense and economic rehabilitation on American help. In both
cases, it is one dominant power which exercises leadership over
a large number of countries.

In the case of the Western world, this leadership presents a
large number of new problems. The United States cannot and
would not "buy" the co-operation of European countries. Still
less does it consider machinery of coercion. It depends to a large
extent on the creation of understanding and good will. Whatever parts of the world this country co-ordinates in the "American Century," it has to do much of its work by devices of long-
distance communication. Anyone who has watched the growth
of the U. S. Information Services in various countries and has
compared them with the embassies of twenty years ago will
have a good picture of this new situation. In virtually every
capital in the world, the United States makes available books or
films or magazines, giving the educated people in each country
information on the United States. And virtually every United
States embassy staff includes a few trained social scientists,
whose job it is to give Washington a competent picture of the
territory in which they serve. The radio programs of the Voice
of America are another example of the network of mass communications which is spread over many thousands of square
miles. If the parallel is not too far-fetched, it might be permissible to say that, while the British Empire discharged its trustee-
ship through the proverbial colonial civil servant, the "American Empire" does so through the help of its information and
communications officers.

Nor has this development been confined to the international
scene. We have watched it in connection with national matters
for several decades. The Pinkerton detective who clubbed down
a strike fifty years ago has been replaced by the labor relations
expert who tries to keep workers' morale high. Fifty years ago
the lobbyist tried to get the support of individual legislators;

today, added to this, we have institutional advertising and public relations experts who try to create good will among the larger public. Thus coercion is being displaced by influence; and influence is becoming an increasingly intricate combination of face-to-face contacts and the skillful use of the mass media of communication.

New forms of social organization call for new developments in social knowledge. It would not be difficult to show that the problems of the British colonial administration gave considerable impetus to the development of anthropology. It was found, for instance, that well-intentioned administrative measures led to considerable social disorganization among the native populations. Out of such experiences grew the whole concept of "functionalism," the idea that one part of a social system cannot be changed without greatly affecting all other parts. There was a strong mutual influence between anthropology as a science and colonial administration as the face-to-face contact between representatives of different cultures.

It seems likely that current problems of international integration will have their social science correlate in the rapidly developing discipline of communications research. As a matter of fact, it is quite possible that the rapid development of this field is partly the result of a vague feeling that the American Century will need exactly this kind of knowledge. Many observers who travel in Europe or Latin America report how strongly people's images of America are determined by the Hollywood motion pictures that they see. Probably the only American materials available to people behind the Iron Curtain are a few thousand copies of the magazine AMERIKA. Practically every United States Information office abroad has a busy lending library for films. The Voice of America may not have a very large audience, but it is probably listened to by opinion-forming sectors of the foreign population.

But what does all this mean? Do these media really influence people? How do we know that many of them don't boomerang, having quite different consequences than those intended by their American sponsors? Who really knows what role the different media play in other countries? More frequent and ever louder are the voices which raise these questions. As a matter of fact, one sometimes has the feeling that bewildered policy makers expect more help from the social scientist than he possibly can give. The anxiety of the administrator is matched by the anxiety of the communications research man; both suddenly find themselves actors on a stage which has grown more rapidly than their own experience and skill.

In such a situation, anything which will enlarge the knowledge of the communications field is highly welcome. The present text is one such contribution. While the literature on communications research is quite extensive, specific books and studies dealing with the motion pictures are relatively rare. This is true for a variety of reasons. For one, there has been less commercial money. The assumption has been that each film presented a new problem, and could not be considered a typical product like daytime serials or successive issues of the same magazine, for example. Then too the executives in the movie industry are probably more individualistic and more distrustful of systematic research than those in any other communication industry. Whatever the reason, only a few motion picture companies, and still fewer research agencies, have studied film products systematically.

This is regrettable, because in what we have become used to calling "backward areas" movies will probably play a considerable role. In this country, people who cannot read, and therefore cannot be reached by print, can listen to the radio. In most foreign countries, however, radio is rarely available outside the metropolitan districts. Large areas are not electrified, and if they are, radio sets are economically beyond the reach of most of the population. In such a situation, the truck which can bring movies to villages and small towns is likely to play a large role. But even in this country, the potential use of movies is less fully exploited than are radio and print, both of which have pretty well saturated their markets. While it is not yet clear what the future of the 16-millimeter film and the documentary will be, there seems to be little doubt that an increasing number of organizations, libraries, and schools are making use of them at the present time.

Leo Handel's book brings current movie research up to date. In its organization, the field is similar to the more conventional aspects of radio or magazine research. The book outlines how the size of movie audiences is measured, how people's preferences are ascertained, and it summarizes the little we know about the effect of films. It gives us the opportunity to see certain peculiar aspects of film research. For instance, the effects of motion pictures have been studied relatively well. This is due to the fact that in specific situations movies have become either especially controversial or especially important. An example of the former case are the studies which were done twenty years ago on the effect of movies on children. An instance of the latter situation is exemplified by the extensive use which the Army made of indoctrination films; it led to a series of experimental studies which are probably the most detailed in any field of mass communications. On the other hand, the attitude of the movie audience is probably less well explored than the attitude of, say, the listeners to daytime serials or the readers of comic books.

Leo Handel is probably the only full-time audience research director employed by a major motion picture company. His experience, therefore, is rather unique in the commercial field, and he has drawn particularly on commercial research data available only to him. But he has also surveyed and integrated into his text the more complex work done in non-commercial research.

The reader will not find in this text any attempt to connect film research with the broader social and political problems of our time. But he would probably find it nowhere. This brings up a final and very important point of view from which a text like the present one should be viewed. We do not yet have any real integration of communications research and the broader concepts and problems of the social sciences. This is partly due to the youth of the whole communications field. But it is still more due to an unfortunate separation of experience and training. The general social scientist does not yet know the findings of the communications research student; the practitioner of communications research often has no training in the general social sciences. This makes a new text in the field so important. By reading this book, not only the practitioner, but also the social scientist, can for the first time get a good picture of where communications research stands in the field of motion pictures. It is hoped that he will apply his own thinking and his own problems to the data and techniques presented here. The result should be a quicker integration of this new field with the general stream of social research. The content of the present text will speak for itself. The introduction intends to speak for the diversified and creative uses to which the book can be put.

Columbia University   PAUL F. LAZARSFELD
March, 1950

CONTENTS

Part One: The industry and research. Some fundamental facts of film audience research

CHAPTER 1 *The development and nature of film audience research*

The last ten years have witnessed great strides in many areas of communications research, both in the development of new techniques of measurement and in the accumulation of empirical data. Ingenious methods and devices for studying radio listeners have been developed which are utilized now, to some extent, for analyses of television audiences. Magazine, book, and newspaper readers have been subjected to increasing scrutiny. A considerable body of information has been gathered which is useful not only to workers in these specific branches of communication but also to social researchers in general.

Film audience research on the whole has lagged behind research in the other mass media. What little had been done before the forties was largely financed by educational funds and was primarily concerned with the educational aspects of motion pictures. Thus, at a time when radio, newspaper, and magazine audience research was an accepted institution, financed by the private organizations most directly concerned, film audience research was confined to a few isolated attempts.

The reasons for the slow start of motion picture research are manifold. The young industry, which could readily finance research projects, found little motivation to do so because the

3

new, expanding market was active enough to provide a highly satisfactory volume of business for the leading firms. Most motion picture executives were content to let product improvement and sales policies rest on their intuitive insight of what the public wanted, rather than on direct contact with the consumer. Some members of the industry, moreover, received the impression that research threatened to constitute itself as an independent authority and resented possible interference with their own power. They saw in audience research not an instrument for their use, but a substitute for their executive acumen. Also, the film industry had developed its own quasi-scientific instruments to gauge public opinion, which were considered to be of sufficient reliability. Some of these industry-created methods will be discussed presently.

Just before the outbreak of World War II the use and development of film audience research began to accelerate, possibly because intuition proved less and less infallible at the box-office as the expansion of the industry approached the saturation point, and probably also because consumer research had become a *fait accompli* in other fields. At this time, Audience Research, Inc., was organized by George Gallup and began to serve a number of motion picture firms, including some independent producers. The author's Motion Picture Research Bureau began operating for various firms, and since 1942 has conducted studies exclusively for Metro-Goldwyn-Mayer except for an interruption of three years while the author served with the Army.

World War II itself brought further development of film research due to the activities of the Research Branch of the War Department. This special agency was established partly for the purpose of determining the effects of orientation films to be released to the armed forces. The valuable contribution to research made by this unit will be described later.

Eric Johnston gave impetus to movie research when he established in 1946 a Department of Research within the Motion Picture Association of America, under the directorship of Robert W. Chambers. The objective was (1) to correct possible misinformation of the public and to eliminate the guesswork which had characterized industry statistics, (2) to engage in research projects designed to furnish the industry with scientific data as a basis for the formation of policy, and (3) to undertake special studies concerning the value of the motion picture as a cultural force.

In England the first contribution to film audience research was made by Sidney L. Bernstein, through the Granada Theatres, Ltd. Bernstein's extensive work included studies of younger moviegoers. The chief difference between the British and American approaches is that the British mainly use questionnaires which are filled in by the respondents, while the Americans mainly conduct personal interviews.

These developments, along with the continuing studies of educational groups, resulted in a considerable body of information; but so far no attempt had been made to present the findings, to outline the problems, or to conduct research in a systematic fashion. To indicate the breadth of the field of "film audience research" it might be well to indicate some points of view from which such audience studies have been made.

One type of study concerns itself with the characteristics of the moviegoing public as compared with the infrequent or nonmoviegoers. A division may be made between "regular," "occasional," and "non-moviegoers." The focus of such studies is on the difference in background characteristics of the different classes of audiences. Another way of classifying studies is that which relates them to the structure of motion picture concerns, and consequently divides the work into:

(a) Production research
(b) Distribution (sales) research
(c) Promotion (advertising, publicity, and exploitation) research
(d) Exhibition (theater) research

The psychologist working in this field would be apt to organize his studies in a manner such as this:

(a) Studies of audience reactions and gratifications
(b) Studies of the effectiveness of films

(c) Content analysis of motion pictures
(d) Studies of the structure of the motion picture audience

For the purposes of this volume the following primary division has been used, largely influenced by the availability of material:

(a) Studies pertaining to specific motion picture productions
(b) Studies dealing with general film audience research problems

Part II, which is devoted to research concerning specific productions, describes studies conducted at various stages through which motion pictures pass: the pretesting of the story, the selection of players and title, the testing and evaluation of the finished product, and the research co-ordinated with selling and advertising.

The second group of studies pertaining to general problems is described in Part III, and covers the investigations of the audience itself, its size, composition and behavior, its general preferences for story types and players. Included here are also studies pertaining to content analysis, to the effect of movies. The relation of movies to other branches of communications and the theater itself are also part of this section.

EVALUATIVE STUDIES BY THE INDUSTRY

As stated before, the motion picture industry has for some time been employing, to some extent, a number of methods other than consumer research to gauge audience reactions. The following section shows briefly the potentialities and limitations of such evaluative measurements as analysis of box-office returns, sneak previews, fan mail analysis, gauging of exhibitor opinions, and theatrical tryouts.

ANALYSIS OF BOX-OFFICE RETURNS

The selling practices of the motion picture industry underwent considerable changes while films evolved from the flicker stage into one of the most powerful means of mass communication. At one time it was the policy to sell a combination of a feature and a short subject to the exhibitor in a fixed program without his knowing in advance what he would receive. After that came the period of group (star or series) selling when exhibitors bought "blocks" of pictures which sometimes made it necessary to take inferior productions along with good ones. Only recently has the industry begun to rent individual pictures independently of other commitments. In this last stage some analysis of public acceptance became of increasing importance, since it was now necessary to evaluate each picture separately to determine its drawing power and set a policy for its rental.

To establish a criterion for setting the rental policy for a picture, for instance, it has become customary to show it before its general release in a number of test localities. The revenues obtained in these first engagements are used as an important lead in the estimation of the sales potential. More specifically, the box-office returns in these index cities determine the percentage bracket into which a picture falls in respect to the "rental" exhibitors will be asked to pay to the distributor. For the majority of pictures the rental amounts to from 20 per cent to 40 per cent of the intake at the box-office. There are, however, pictures which are sold under "special" arrangements and on sliding scales, in which the exhibitors rental may exceed 40 per cent.[1] A picture that proves to be successful during the test engagements is thus given every opportunity for favorable audience exposure and for topflight exploitation.

Box-office figures, whether they represent a single test engagement or the eventual total revenue of a picture, are the result of many factors. These factors embrace the intrinsic quality of the picture, the volume and effectiveness of advertising and publicity preceding and coincidental with the picture's release, the popularity of all the players appearing in the film, and the appeal of the title. Seasonal influences are also at work, as is the weather. Competitive pictures, the general success of contemporary films, and the position with regard to a film cycle (if the picture can be so categorized) have an effect at the box-office.

---

[1] The distributor has no jurisdiction over theater admissions since the courts have ruled that it is illegal to attempt controlling admission prices.

There is also the presence of counter-attractions other than motion pictures. In the case of double features or stage shows it is difficult to determine accurately the revenues for each attraction.

Box-office returns are therefore a measurement of the over-all performance of a motion picture. But an analysis of the box-office figures becomes inconclusive when it purports to measure and isolate any of the above elements. Sometimes an attempt is made to determine the drawing power of different titles by showing a picture under different titles in various localities. It hardly can be assured that reliable control conditions will prevail in the respective trial towns; and without identical basic conditions the results obtained are of doubtful value. The same holds true probably for the testing of different promotional campaigns in various territories.

Box-office returns are used also to gauge the popularity of players. This practice may have some justification in the case of a picture which is built around one star only. But if more than one star appears in the film, revenues do not indicate the share of success due to any single player.

It will be shown later that research procedures make it possible to isolate the various elements conglomerated in the box-office revenues.

SNEAK PREVIEWS

The theory behind the sneak preview comes close to sound research. In some cases, however, the actual execution of determining audience reactions in that way is not as reliable as it could be.

After the completion of a motion picture, a print of it is often taken to a theater in or near Los Angeles and shown to a supposedly typical paying audience of moviegoers. Members of the production staff attend the performance to feel out the audience's reception of the picture. After the screening of the test film, preview cards may be distributed among the spectators, who are invited to jot down their opinions of the picture and to mail the card to the producer. One shortcoming of this

method is that such sneak previews are not always attended by
typical audiences; even if they are held at a location quite
distant from the studio, they are apt to be attended by too many
persons who have some personal interest in the production. The
impressions obtained during such performances are often used
to make changes, retakes, or cuts in the picture. More often they
cause the omission of changes, retakes, or cuts which might have
appeared to be advisable had the very same print been shown to
a really impartial movie audience.

Another inadequacy of Hollywood sneak previews is that they
do not, unless accidentally, represent a satisfactory cross-section
of the movie audience. No effort is made to stratify the respondents. Usually there is no way of determining the classification
data of the person who filled in the cards and it is impossible to
tell how closely the test audience corresponds to the general
moviegoing audience. On one occasion, the respondents were
asked to indicate their sex on the cards. Of the 326 cards which
were mailed in, 108 were filled in by men, 185 by women, and
33 failed to indicate their sex. Obviously, these replies were un-
balanced, since we know that about as many men as women attend movies in America, and we also know that preferences
differ between the sexes.

Another shortcoming of uncontrolled sneak previews may
be that persons who like the picture are more apt to fill in the
cards than people who did not like it. Even though no experiments to this effect have been conducted in movie research, it
may be assumed that the same criterion holds true for preview
cards as for mail surveys in general. Analyses have revealed that
persons who are more interested in the subject matter are proportionately better represented in the returns than those who
do not show any interest in it. Furthermore, the opinions expressed on preview cards do not lend themselves very easily to
tabulation.

Sneak previews, little value though they may seem to have for
the professional researcher, were a step in the direction of more
scientific and more reliable methods which will be outlined in
a later chapter.

FAN MAIL ANALYSIS

Fan mail comes into Hollywood's studios daily by the truck-load. A conservative estimate puts the letters addressed to play-ers at a quarter of a million a month. A top star expects about three thousand a week. So the stars of filmdom eye with great concern the flow of fan mail directed to them.[2] The studios to which they are under contract carefully measure and weigh the amount of fan mail every player receives. They deduce from its increase or decrease a rise or fall in the popularity of the recipient. This again is only a very rough approach to measur-ing the drawing power of players. One important point should not be overlooked in the consideration of fan mail analysis. Only a small section of the moviegoing public indulges in the writing of fan mail. It is largely teen-agers and young girls who seek this contact with their favorite stars; the rank and file of moviegoers is not fully represented. Therefore, conclusions based on fan mail cannot be taken as the final word because such mail is not produced by the typical cross-section on which reliable research bases its findings.

EVALUATION OF EXHIBITOR OPINIONS

The exhibitor is, in a sense, the link between movie producer and moviegoer. His opinion is a double factor in the marketing of a motion picture because he must first be convinced of its value before he will become a purchaser, and subsequently must be sufficiently interested in the production to give it a good publicity and advertising campaign. Exhibitor opinions are voiced during conventions, in trade papers, and in an ample and carefully supervised correspondence with the motion picture companies. The exhibitor's point of view is discussed during conferences with the distributor's sales staff in the field. Gen-erally exhibitor opinions and recommendations are very con-

[2] Thorp (*America at the Movies*, Yale University, 1939) writes that a student of the American language once made an exhaustive study of the vocabulary of these constant writers. Each writer, he found, has at his command, for the ex-pression of the whole gamut of rapture and disgust, just one hundred and fifty words.

structive but, like other people, exhibitors can be subject to biased ideas which they may groundlessly assume are shared by their patrons. Preferences or dislikes, too, observed and reported by one exhibitor, may prevail only in his location. Also, in some respects exhibitors and distributors are pursuing divergent interests, the natural divergence of interests in the seller and buyer relationship.

THEATRICAL TRYOUTS

The motion picture industry has had for some time the policy of buying film rights to plays. These plays may be staged in one of the large Broadway houses or by stock companies on the road. Audience reactions are studied very carefully and may help in deciding whether or not the play property should be made into a motion picture. Some film producers have sent companies and writers on the road to try out intended movies as stage shows.

Here, again, a question must be raised as to the reliability of the procedure. It is probable that the audience of most plays is very different in social composition from the audience of most motion pictures, and the basis of popularity for the two types of presentations would be quite different. Then, too, plays can be shown in only limited localities, and movies have wide distribution.

CHAPTER *2* *Some problems of film*

audience research

Audience research undertaken for the motion picture industry in connection with specific problems of feature production, distribution, and promotion offers certain problems, some of them of a rather unique nature.

One of the most pronounced features of this sort of research is the speed with which it must be carried out. Studies conducted before the production must be turned out rapidly because the producer usually is anxious to establish his plans. It is obvious that studies which are conducted for a picture while it is in the shooting stage have to be executed speedily to keep in step with the production.

Sometimes there is only a short time between the completion of the release prints and their national distribution. The completed picture constitutes a large investment for the producing company and its financial backers. The average studio negative costs of the pictures produced in the United States amounted to $1,028,240 in 1948.[1] Actually the producing budgets range from $100,000 for inexpensive B pictures (usually Westerns with location shots) to $4,000,000 and more for a major production.

[1] *Film Daily Year Book of Motion Pictures*, 1949, p. 67.

The necessity for speedy amortization and turnover of such
investment is obvious.

From all this it can be readily seen that an audience research
unit working for the industry has to be set up in such a way that
assignments can be carried out speedily. In case of need it
should be able to execute them within twenty-four to forty-
eight hours. To do so it is necessary to have special arrangements with a nationwide staff of field investigators capable of
receiving instructions by wire or telephone and, after com-
pleting their assignments, phoning or wiring back the results
obtained.

Another aspect of a great many studies of the motion picture
audience is the fact that the respondents have no clear con-
ception, before the interviews, of the issue about which they are
to be questioned. In some other fields of research the consumer's
preferences and dislikes may be fairly easily established, for he
has had experience with the product, or a product of a very
similar type, before. Most people have a very definite idea as to
their favorite brand of cigarettes, their favorite canned soup,
or their favorite radio program. In the case of film audience
research, however, the line of questioning may embrace a topic
entirely new to the interviewee. For this reason many motion
picture interviews must be executed in *two steps*. The first is
to familiarize the respondent with the problem at hand. Only
during the second part of the interview does the actual questioning begin and the respondent is asked to state his opinion
or preference, as the case may be.

Title tests are an example of this method. The first step is to
familiarize the respondent with the titles under investigation.
For this purpose the interviewee is usually exposed to an audio-
visual impression. He is given a checklist showing the titles
while the enumerator reads them to him. The second step is to
let the respondent select the title which is the most attractive
to him.

Another problem of film audience research is the effect of
the last exposure to the medium, or the carry-over of the last
movie visit. This influence can be positive or negative and is

usually quite obvious, especially in star popularity polls. In case an open-ended question is asked to determine the favorite movie star of a group of respondents, a large proportion of them will name the players they saw in the last picture they liked well. The questions and answers would often develop in the following manner:

Question: "Who is your favorite star?"
Answer: "I think it is Star X, the fellow I saw in the picture 'A' last night."

The use of checklists from which the respondent can choose his favorite stars eliminates to some extent the influence of the last attendance.

Still another source of difficulty in film audience research is the lack of continuity of the motion picture medium. A picture, as a rule, is seen just once. Trends in motion picture tastes are therefore more difficult to measure than, for example, the audience reaction to a radio program. The latter shows up clearly in an increased or decreased audience volume in subsequent broadcasts of the same program, while the former lacks an identical basis of comparison.

While discussing the difficulties film audience investigations have to cope with as compared to some other branches of research, we must not neglect mentioning the excellent co-operation field investigators are given by the respondents. In most cases only moviegoers are interviewed. They are interested and eager to answer questions pertaining to motion pictures. This co-operative spirit in the field is very valuable and most encouraging for the field staff.

THE "WANT-TO-SEE" QUESTION

The "want-to-see" question is a device quite frequently used in film audience research. Eventually it may also find some prominence in television audience investigations. We will find in later chapters that this type of question may be employed for evaluating the appeal of a story theme, the marquee value of a player, the drawing power of a title, and the effect of an advertising campaign. The appeal of an entire picture may be measured by testing the combined drawing power of its component parts—cast, theme, and title.

On the surface the "want-to-see" question is a concise and straightforward form of interrogation. Questions, such as the following, seem to offer a few obstacles:

"Would you want to see a picture if you knew nothing about it except that Clark Gable is playing a leading part in it?"

Actually the "want-to-see" questions present one of the more intricate problems of motion picture audience research. To the author's knowledge no analytical work has been done to obtain a greater insight in this matter. The following, therefore, is more an outline of suggestions for future studies than a report on accomplished research.

First of all the "want-to-see" question is not always what it purports to be. It may be phrased in different ways and, consequently, yield different results. Here are a few examples of phrasings which may be employed:

"Do you want to go and see . . . ."
"Are you interested in seeing . . . ."
"Would you buy a ticket for . . . ."
"Would you yourself buy a ticket for . . . ."
"Would you yourself buy a ticket or ask the person you go with to buy one . . . ."

A number of comparative studies demonstrated that the number of affirmative answers to a "want-to-see" question decreases if the questions are more specific. A brief example of a test will illustrate this statement.

An attempt was made to determine the popularity of a motion picture star by three different ways of questioning. In each case a sample of five hundred New York moviegoers was used. In Table 1 are the three different questions and the tabulations of the returns. The name of the player must be withheld.

The straight "want-to-see" question, a very general form of inquiry, draws general answers. There is a difference between just *wanting* to see a picture and the definite impulse for actual attendance. If the question becomes more specific and it is asked whether the respondent would actually *go and see* the picture the number of affirmative answers decreased. "Would you yourself *buy* a ticket" is another step toward greater specificity. The association of the movie visit with the necessary money outlay thus brought the lowest returns.

TABLE 1

POPULARITY OF STAR X

	Yes	No	Don't know	Total
1. *Would you want to see* a picture about which you knew only that Star X is playing in the lead?	51%	43%	6%	100%
2. *Would you go and see* a picture about which you knew only that Star X is playing the lead?	45	47	8	100
3. *Would you yourself buy* a ticket for a picture about which you knew only that Star X is playing the lead?	37	52	11	100

It may be argued that this sort of question has a drawback in that many persons who go to the movies do not pay for their own tickets. But these persons may have been the driving power behind a movie visit and may have also been responsible for the attendance of other persons even though they answered negatively the question "Would *you yourself* buy a ticket. . . ?" It should be also noted that the proportion of "don't knows" increases with the greater specificity of the question.

Another problem pertaining to the "want-to-see" question is created by what might be called the nonselective audience. This type of moviegoer answers most "want-to-see" questions in the affirmative. A characteristic reaction from an indiscriminating moviegoer to a "want-to-see" question about a picture would be:

I see practically every picture my theater (respondent's neighborhood house) shows during the weekend, regardless of what is playing. I certainly would see the picture you ask me about if it were playing there . . . .

The existence of this basic audience of nonselective movie-goers may complicate the analysis, unless we know its exact size and location, for it raises the question of how much of the audience is created by the availability of the picture and how much by the picture's appeal. It has been found, for instance, that there is a larger proportion of nonselective moviegoers in small towns than in large towns. If we are interested in judging the *appeal* of a particular picture, therefore, we must give more weight to the figures from the larger communities. For the purpose of determining potential ticket sales, however, the non-selective audience need not be eliminated from the analysis.

To mention another difficulty encountered in the application of the "want-to-see" question, the proportion of moviegoers answering affirmatively to even careful phrasing of the question is frequently higher than the proportion of persons who would actually go and see the picture under investigation. The title, cast, and story for many "A" pictures would draw "want-to-see" percentages ranging between 50 and 70 per cent of a sample of moviegoers, whereas the actual attendance figures would be lower. The reasons may be many. Some persons wanting to see the picture may not be in a position to do so when the picture is shown in their town or in their neighborhood and they may not be willing to go to another neighborhood to see it. Another reason may be found in the competitive situation. Coincident with the picture that has been tested, another one with a higher audience appeal may be shown in the same neighborhood which the moviegoer would choose to see. Also, the effect of advertis-ing will have a decided influence on the potential patrons, as will negative word-of-mouth publicity. The results of "want-to-see" tests should, therefore, be seen in relation to returns from other tests rather than as an absolute prediction.

Another factor observed is the close range of "want-to-see" figures for different stars, titles, stories, and their combinations. An example of these relations is presented in the chapter "Title

Tests." The usual range for the average "A" picture was also mentioned above.[2] To obtain valid results in comparison tests it is, therefore, necessary to use large samples to minimize the statistical margin of error.

The relevance of the points outlined in this chapter will be seen more clearly in the subsequent pages where concrete studies are discussed.

[2] According to Audience Research, Inc., the average "want-to-see" (the percentage of filmgoers who definitely desire to buy a ticket for a picture after learning its cast, title, and story theme) for the average "A" picture was 56 per cent between 1943 and 1947, and 53 per cent in 1948 (*Variety*, February 23, 1949).

Part Two: Studies of individual productions

CHAPTER *3 Tests before production begins*

There are two main points at which audience research can help the motion picture producer before the production of a film has begun. It may assist him, in the first place, in determining what stories or plots are likely to have a wide appeal among his potential audience. Secondly, research can discover which of the available actors the moviegoers would most like to see in certain roles.

STORY TESTS

Stories and plots for motion pictures are drawn from many different sources. The majority of today's screenfare is based on original screen stories. Many other pictures, especially important high-budgeted productions, are film versions of current bestsellers and Broadway plays.

Table 2 shows the various sources of material for feature-length pictures.[1]

The industry invests a great deal of capital in story material of each of these main types. The following figures, referring to story transactions in 1945, reflect the importance of this phase of production.

[1] Data supplied by the Motion Picture Association of America.

TABLE 2

SOURCE MATERIAL OF FEATURE-LENGTH PICTURES
APPROVED BY PRODUCTION CODE ADMINISTRATION
1935–48 [1]

Year	Original screen stories		Stage plays		Novels		Biographies		Short stories		Source unknown		Miscellaneous [3]	
	Number	Per cent	Number	Per cent	Number	Per cent	Number	Per cent	Number	Per cent	Number	Per cent	Number	Per cent
1935 [2]	244	47.0	41	7.9	142	27.4	3	.6	37	7.1	28	5.4	24	4.6
1936 [2]	371	67.8	38	7.0	92	16.8	2	.4	39	7.1	...	...	5	.9
1937	391	64.3	39	6.4	102	16.8	12	2.0	46	7.6	11	1.8	7	1.1
1938	316	58.0	30	5.5	140	25.7	2	.4	54	9.9	...	...	3	.5
1939	329	56.3	34	5.8	127	21.8	17	2.9	59	10.1	10	1.7	8	1.4
1940	323	61.8	51	9.8	109	20.8	8	1.5	21	4.0	...	...	11	2.1
1941	358	63.0	57	10.0	58	10.2	4	.7	82	14.5	5	.9	4	.7
1942	401	73.4	31	5.7	57	10.4	7	1.3	29	5.3	8	1.5	13	2.4
1943	312	74.8	23	5.5	42	10.0	2	.5	6	1.4	16	3.9	16	3.9
1944	321	72.6	28	6.3	48	10.9	2	.5	10	2.3	9	2.0	24	5.4
1945	251	64.5	26	6.7	59	15.2	...	...	10	2.6	2	.5	41	10.5
1946	259	60.9	22	5.2	65	15.3	1	.2	10	2.4	5	1.2	63	14.8
1947	233	57.7	17	4.2	87	21.5	...	...	5	1.2	10	2.5	52	12.9
1948	244	56.1	26	6.0	76	17.5	2	.4	23	5.3	10	2.3	54	12.4
	4,353	62.6	463	6.7	1,204	17.3	62	.9	431	6.2	114	1.6	325	4.7

[1] Does not include pictures reissued.
[2] Data for this year include pictures approved in Hollywood office only.
[3] Including such sources as comic strips, radio programs, nonfiction, travelogues, poems, etc.

Story purchases by the Hollywood studios amounted to an estimated $6,413,200 in 1947.[2]

Top prices for books were obtained in 1945 for Somerset Maugham's *The Razor's Edge,* acquired by Twentieth Century-Fox, and Adria Locke Langley's *A Lion Is in the Streets,* acquired by William Cagney Productions. The producers paid $250,000 for each of these novels.

The highest price for a produced Broadway play was paid by Warner Brothers, who acquired John Van Druten's "The Voice of the Turtle" for $500,000 on a profit-sharing arrangement.

The original screen story which drew the highest price in 1945 was "I've Always Loved You" by Border Chase which was bought by Republic for $100,000.

With so much at stake, it is obviously of interest to movie producers to discover, through whatever research techniques can be applied, which story themes are likely to arouse the most interest or, more specifically, which will be likely to bring the largest numbers of people into the movie houses. Tests may be conducted to measure the appeal of single original screen stories, or ideas for stories, or to help decide between two or more stories under consideration.

The nucleus of a story test for an original story is a synopsis which is shown to the respondents in the field. This is not so much a description of the plot in detail as of broad aspects of the subject matter. The descriptions usually condense the story material to about sixty words. The following are two examples of brief summaries which were actually used by Audience Research, Inc.[3]

THE DARK MIRROR. When a wealthy society doctor is murdered, the police know a beautiful girl, easily identified, murdered him. But when the girl turns out to have an identical twin sister, the police don't know which one is guilty and which to arrest. A young doctor analyzes their personalities, falls in love with one and discovers which is the murderess.

[2] This figure, and amounts stated for story acquisitions, are quoted from the *Film Daily Year Book of Motion Pictures,* 1946 and 1948.

[3] *Screen Writer,* March, 1947, p. 34.

CORNERED. Fresh from the war, Pete goes on a manhunt to avenge his brother's death. The trail leads to Mocha Joe's West Indies Cabaret. Injuries have changed Joe's features but Pete recognizes him as the murderer. Cunningly he plays cat-and-mouse with his dangerous enemy. Then Pete falls in love with Joe's beautiful, unhappy wife and . . . .

To give a better idea of the steps involved in a story test, we might describe in some detail one such study which was conducted in connection with the production of the story of the atomic bomb in film.

The title selected for this picture was "The Beginning or the End." Company executives were anxious to anticipate to some extent the attitude of the moviegoing public toward this rather out-of-the-ordinary project.

In December, 1945, when the study was made, only the work title and a rough idea of the general theme were available. The cast had not been selected, but it was assumed that the studio would supply its most qualified talent for this production.

The survey was conducted on a nationwide scale. About 2,000 interviews were recorded with persons who had attended motion pictures at least once within the month prior to the interview.[4]

To give the respondents a basis for judgment, a brief outline of the basic idea was printed on a card as follows:

> This picture will show in the form of an exciting story how the release of atomic energy will affect you and your family—whether this most important invention of all times will be the beginning of a better world, or the end of everything. The picture will have an all-star cast and its title will be:
>
> "THE BEGINNING OR THE END"

The interviewers read this brief outline to the respondents while they themselves were reading the card in order to expose them to a simultaneous audio-visual impression. To measure the respondents' degree of interest in the subject matter they

[4] The author is indebted to Metro-Goldwyn-Mayer for the release of these figures.

were handed a checklist with the scaled statements: *Very in-teresting, Fairly interesting, Slightly interesting, Not at all in-teresting.* They were asked the question: "How interesting would this picture be to you?" It will be noticed that men and women felt very much the same on the subject.

TABLE 3

QUESTION: HOW INTERESTING WOULD THIS PICTURE BE TO YOU?

	Men	Women	Total
Very interesting	62%	61%	62%
Fairly interesting	22	22	22
Slightly interesting	7	9	8
Not at all interesting	9	8	8
Total	100%	100%	100%

After the respondents selected the interest intensity which fitted or came nearest to their own evaluation, the question which was of greatest concern to the producing company was put before them:

TABLE 4

QUESTION: DO YOU THINK YOU WILL ACTUALLY GO AND SEE THIS PICTURE?

	Men	Women	Total
Yes	73%	71%	72%
No	10	10	10
Undecided	17	19	18
Total	100%	100%	100%

These figures constituted an unusually high anticipation level of the audience. However, the survey contained a bias which was not eliminated. Atomic energy has been one of the principal topics of discussion since the bombing of Hiroshima. Every intelligent person is expected to show active interest in its potentialities. Doubtless many respondents who actually did not care to see a picture on this subject answered affirmatively just because they did not want to seem uninformed and un-concerned about so important a matter.

When this study was prepared it might have been well to attempt to eliminate or at least reduce this bias. One way might have been the insertion of an initial question to divide the audience into moviegoers who *are* and who *are not* basically interested in actually seeing such a picture on the screen. The respondents might have been approached with some such question as:

We all realize the importance of the discovery of the atom bomb and the release of atomic energy in general. What we would like to find out here is whether or not you would care to have this problem brought up in an entertainment film?

In this case the interviewer is making it quite clear from the beginning that he is taking for granted that the respondent is interested in this issue. The question is reduced to the simple alternative of whether or not the respondent wants to have it treated *in a picture*. The interviewee can answer "No" without losing face.

There is another sort of difficulty with this technique of analysis from plot synopsis that would apply not only to our example here but to any such analysis. This arises from the impossibility of writing a synopsis that will not bias to some extent the distribution of responses. For the same picture two synopses could be written that would result in entirely different acceptance ratings.

Robert Shaw, in the article "A Package Deal in Film Opinions" [5] wonders how such a film as "Brief Encounter" would have fared if it had been submitted to an audience cross-section using the following story condensation:

An unglamorous housewife living in the suburbs of London meets by chance a middle-aged doctor while she is on a shopping trip to the city. They are attracted to each other. They arrange to meet again, and they innocently enjoy talking, lunching and seeing movies together. Falling deeply in love, she agrees to a night rendezvous. When a coincidence prevents its consummation, he leaves for Africa and she returns to her dull and very decent husband.

[5] *Screen Writer,* March, 1947, p. 34.

An unfavorable audience reception to this synopsis might seem a foregone conclusion, since whatever beauty and tenderness there is in the story has been distilled from it. A different version, however, might have been able to capture some of the story's more appealing qualities.

Next to original scripts, novels, both classics and current bestsellers, are the most important source of motion picture stories.

Producers select novels for different reasons. They are sometimes interested in the story as is, sometimes only in certain parts of it, and sometimes they merely want to take advantage of an attractive and well-publicized title. In still other cases they want to exploit the advance publicity created by the publication of the novel. The names of renowned authors may also be considered important attractions. In many instances a combination of some or most of these considerations will lead to the acquisition of the movie rights of a novel.

Whenever the purchase of the rights of a novel is being weighed, the producer is primarily interested in the answers to the following questions:

How many persons know about the novel?

How many persons read the novel, and how many persons of those who read it would want to see it made into a motion picture?

How many persons who know about the novel without having read it would want to see it filmed?

How many persons who do not know anything about the novel would want to see a picture based on the subject matter?

The application of the survey technique can usually yield much valuable information on these points.

Preparations were started on the motion picture "Jane Eyre," based on Charlotte Brontë's classic of the same title, early in 1941. In the course of the preliminary arrangements, the Motion Picture Research Bureau gathered some background data on the project, based on over 1,800 stratified interviews with persons attending the movies on the average of at least once a month.

Among other things, it was necessary to find out the proportion of moviegoers who had read the book and who would like to see it made into a motion picture.[6]

TABLE 5

QUESTION: DID YOU EVER READ THE BOOK OR DO YOU KNOW THE STORY OF *Jane Eyre?*

	Men	Women	Total
Yes	18%	40%	29%
No	82	60	71
Total	100%	100%	100%

Persons who said they knew the novel were asked if they would like to see it made into a movie.

TABLE 6

QUESTION: WOULD YOU LIKE TO SEE *Jane Eyre* MADE INTO A MOTION PICTURE?

	Men	Women	Total
Yes	89%	95%	93%
No	5	1	2
No difference	6	4	5
Total	100%	100%	100%

Respondents who said they did not know the book were further questioned to determine the appeal of the title "Jane Eyre" to this group of the potential audience.

TABLE 7

QUESTION: WOULD A PICTURE TITLED "JANE EYRE" ATTRACT YOUR INTEREST?

	Men	Women	Total
Yes	37%	49%	42%
No	35	27	32
No opinion	28	24	26
Total	100%	100%	100%

The proportion of persons—42 per cent—who stated they would see the picture just on account of the title "Jane Eyre"

[6] The author is here indebted to Mr. D. O. Selznick for permitting the use of the figures.

may seem rather high to some observers. No detailed analysis of this figure was made at the time of the survey. Other studies, however, indicated that a high "want-to-see" of a title is largely due to indiscriminating moviegoers who "just go and see any picture," regardless of story, cast, title, etc. We will discuss this section of the motion picture audience in more detail later.

The Broadway stage is another important pool from which material for motion pictures is being drawn. The motivation for this policy is similar to the considerations leading to the purchase of the motion picture rights of a novel.

However, there are some important differences. A stage play is more akin to the motion picture medium than to the printed page. The advance publicity that has been given to a play is different from that of a novel. Most plays are staged only in large centers of population; some are shown solely in New York City; others get widespread publicity through stock companies. The circulation figures of a book which is read all over the country in large and small communities must be replaced as a preliminary guide to popularity by the number of admissions in theaters in one or a limited number of localities.

Research studies must, therefore, determine the publicity value of a play at the place or places where it is shown and in communities where it is not shown.

When the Crouse and Lindsay play "Life with Father" started its fourth year in New York, motion picture companies began to show an increasing interest in this successful Broadway hit.

A survey was made to determine the public's awareness of this production. It was of special interest to establish the difference of returns from New York City, where the play experienced its record run, and from other towns where the play was not presented except possibly for some brief road show engagements. The fieldwork was conducted in New York City and five other towns across the country. About six hundred interviews with moviegoers were recorded.

The approach used for this study is often employed in I.Q. tests and other surveys to determine the public's degree of information about a certain subject. The respondents were asked to indicate whether "Life with Father" was a motion picture, a cartoon series, a play, or a book.

Tables 8 and 9 show the tabulation of the answers for New York City (207 interviews) and the other five cities (383 interviews).[7]

TABLE 8

NEW YORK CITY

	Men	Women	Total
"Life with Father" is a:			
Play	82%	82%	82%
Motion picture	7	4	5
Book	9	7	7
Cartoon series	. . .	3	1
Don't know	13	9	11

TABLE 9

FIVE TOWNS

(Not including New York City)

	Men	Women	Total
"Life with Father" is a:			
Play	51%	60%	56%
Motion picture	21	21	21
Book	15	23	19
Cartoon series	12	6	9
Don't know	22	13	17

The degree of information about the play in the two types of communities was thus ascertained as a preliminary step to measuring the value of its advance publicity prior to its production as a movie.

Approaches similar to the ones outlined in the three preceding examples can be used when other media, such as short stories, radio shows, cartoon series, etc., are being acquired for filming purposes.

A novel approach for pretesting motion picture stories (as well as radio scripts, books, and legitimate stage plays) is used

[7] Due to multiple mentions, the percentages in Tables 7 and 8 total more than 100 per cent.

by some research organizations. Even though the technique is still in the experimental stage the results thus far obtained are very encouraging. This method familiarizes a cross-section of respondents with the plot, story type, story development, and psychological make-up of the leading figures. This may be achieved by one of the four following approaches: For the purpose of the study a brief play is written and presented to a cross-section of moviegoers by professional actors (1) in person or (2) by transcription. Or, in a third variation, (3) the story may also be presented in form of narration, or (4) scripts may be distributed to the moviegoers.

In the first three approaches the listeners may express their likes and dislikes simultaneously with the exposure to the story, through the medium of a program analyzer or related apparatus. In all four cases audience reactions are further investigated by intensive interviews. In this way it is attempted to find whether the subject matter, plot and plot development, and the main characters are sufficiently interesting to warrant the production of the picture or to add, change, or eliminate parts of the story.

The psychological interview following the story exposure does not aim merely to establish the likes and dislikes of the story. Instead the respondents are encouraged to voice freely their emotions, mental images, and associations which formed in their minds during the reading or transcription. What people take with them from the movie theater is a feeling of satisfaction, or frustration of their basic emotional needs. The objective of these depth interviews is to determine whether the story has such basic satisfactions to offer and, if so, to find out their nature. An attempt is also made to discover which elements of the story were apt to support, and which were apt to hamper, the over-all satisfaction derived from it.

The field of pretesting offers a fascinating challenge to the practicing researcher. The preceding paragraphs are but a scant outline of what may become a major and highly specialized field of research in the not too distant future.

CASTING AND CASTING COMBINATION TESTS

The leading motion picture companies and independent producers have a large pool of players at their disposal. They must search for vehicles which would suit their principal stars or select the best possible cast for motion picture properties already acquired. In this part of the chapter we are concerned with the selection of stars for screen stories.

Casting tests can be of value to a producer or a director who has more than one star under consideration and available for a certain part in a motion picture. The first part of the test consists either of finding respondents who are already familiar with the story and the parts for which the stars in question are being considered, or of familiarizing the interviewees with the story and the roles for which players are to be selected. Only a group of respondents thoroughly familiar with the background of the story and the main characters can render an intelligent opinion. Discovering the distribution of choices of the stars suggested for a particular part is then the second step in the survey.

Casting combination tests are similar to casting tests. There are three ways of handling them. Which of the techniques is the most advantageous in each case depends upon the stars under consideration, and upon the story.

One way is to select the stars for every part separately, in the manner described before. Another method which is usually used when one of two parts is more important than the other, is to select first the actor who would have the greatest appeal in the leading role, and then show the respondent a list of possible co-stars and have him choose the one which he thinks would be best. The interviewees can also be shown two groups of players —for example, one group of actors and one group of actresses— and select the two he feels would make the most attractive pair.

Both a casting and a casting combination test were part of the previously cited "Jane Eyre" Pre-Production Survey. Four male and four female stars were under consideration.

Both persons who had previously shown (Table 5) they were familiar with the story of *Jane Eyre* were asked first to select their choice for the holder of the title role from among Joan Fontaine, Vivien Leigh, Katharine Hepburn, and Geraldine Fitzgerald.

TABLE 10 [1]

QUESTION: WHICH OF THE FOLLOWING STARS WOULD YOU LIKE BEST IN THE TITLE ROLE?

	Men	Women	Total
Joan Fontaine	26%	30%	28%
Vivien Leigh	24	21	22
Katharine Hepburn	15	23	20
Geraldine Fitzgerald	16	12	13
No preference, other	19	14	17
Total	100%	100%	100%

[1] Based on 536 interviews.

Joan Fontaine registered as first preference in eleven of the twelve cities where the survey was conducted. Her lead seemed therefore validated even though it was not very substantial in percentage.

In the next question, the respondents were asked whom they wanted to play opposite the leading lady they had previously selected. The actors to choose from were Ronald Colman, Walter Pidgeon, James Stephenson, and Alan Marshal.

TABLE 11 [1]

QUESTION: WHICH OF THE FOLLOWING ACTORS WOULD YOU LIKE TO SEE CO-STARRED?

	Men	Women	Total
Ronald Colman	31%	40%	37%
Walter Pidgeon	21	22	21
James Stephenson	11	10	10
Alan Marshal	9	8	8
No preference, other	28	20	24
Total	100%	100%	100%

[1] Based on 536 interviews.

The favorite casting combination was Joan Fontaine and Ronald Colman. Table 12 shows the possible casting combinations, and their respective preference ratings.

The results of the cross tabulation which are presented in Table 12 show the expected result. Ronald Colman and Joan Fontaine, who both lead in their respective categories, were first choice. Vivien Leigh who was trailing Joan Fontaine (Table 10) is moving up even more closely in the correlation table. The best casting combination from the vantage point of the average moviegoer can be isolated in this way. It is then up to the producer to reconcile the more expensive stars with the higher audience appeal they carry.[8]

TABLE 12

PREFERENCE RATINGS OF CASTING COMBINATIONS

	Actresses				
	Fontaine	Leigh	Hepburn	Fitzgerald	Total mentions
Actors					
Ronald Colman	16%	14%	13%	7%	50%
Walter Pidgeon	10	5	8	4	27
James Stephenson	5	2	2	4	13
Alan Marshal	4	2	3	1	10
Total mentions	35%	23%	26%	16%	100%

Casting and story tests can be conducted for producers, directors, or other members of a producing unit. And the purpose of such tests is not to compete with the judgment of men who make pictures, but to supplement it. If, for artistic reasons, a less popular story is considered for a motion picture, producers and directors should not be discouraged from going ahead with it. If a new star is rising, he should be given full opportunity to develop, even if casting tests may show a preference for a name that is already well accepted. The result of a research study is not the final word in a motion picture production, but it should be a guide.

[8] "Jane Eyre" was released by Twentieth Century-Fox in 1944, with Joan Fontaine in the title role, and Orson Welles as Rochester. Orson Welles had not been considerd for this part at the time when the pre-production test was executed.

TITLE TESTS

Besides the matters of story and cast, both of which may lure people into motion picture houses and both of which, therefore, are apt to be subject of movie audience research, there is the consideration of the title. After the release of a film, another element gains increasing importance: the quality of the production as made known through critics' reviews and word-of-mouth advertising. While this "treatment" cannot be pretested, it appears that the names of outstanding directors and producers constitute a good warranty for the success of a picture. The names of Hitchcock and DeMille draw people into motion picture houses in anticipation of a good production.

Table 13 is based on a survey which was conducted by the Motion Picture Research Bureau in 1943. Approximately 2,700 persons were interviewed in ten sampled theaters in New York City and suburbs. However, only about 1,300 selective moviegoers who came to the theaters with the desire to see any of the nine main features embraced by the study were subject to detailed interrogation.

Even though the title appears as the least important of the three aforementioned basic elements of a motion picture, its influence even on the selective audience, measured in paid admissions, is considerable. Major productions are seen by about fifteen million people. Two per cent of the audience attracted by the title would represent 300,000 admissions or about 130,000 box-office dollars.[1]

The drawing power of the title is correlated with the stars and story of the picture. Its importance increases as the appeal

TABLE 13 [1]

QUESTION: WHEN YOU LEARNED ABOUT THE PICTURE WHAT ONE
THING ABOUT IT MADE YOU WANT TO SEE IT?

	Men	Women	Total
Cast, stars	36%	48%	42%
Story, plot	36	23	30
Title	3	2	3
Other answers	24	13	24
Nothing in particular	5	9	7

[1] Due to multiple mentions, percentages add up to more than 100. More recent studies, as yet incomplete, seem to indicate a slight decrease in the importance of the stars, and an increase in the interest of the story.

of the story and the cast decreases, and vice versa. An attractive title is, therefore, of special importance for pictures featuring new, unknown, or less popular players.

Motion picture producers are very well aware of the importance of titles and they make every effort to find attractive ones. A picture which goes into production is identified by a "work" title. If this title is the one of a successful novel or a well-known play it is, as a rule, never changed, even though some producers tend to overestimate the advance publicity value of these media —especially of the plays.

Usually several titles are under consideration for one motion picture. Up to the present time personal judgment was generally used to decide which of the titles proposed would have the greatest box-office appeal. Research surveys, however, have proved that even the most experienced showmen cannot always select the most attractive title. Due to the correlation between

[1] George Gallup states that a good title can add at least $300,000 to the gross of a picture. Shaw, Robert, "A Package Deal in Film Opinions" *Screen Writer,* March, 1947, p. 36.

title appeal and box-office returns, the industry has become increasingly aware of the possibilities of audience research in this particular field.

Title tests are not necessarily conducted during the actual shooting of the picture, but in most cases the final title is decided upon by the time the production of the picture is completed. For reasons of advance publicity, it is advisable to determine the release title as soon as possible. A large amount of publicity material is disseminated to the radio and to the press when a picture project gets under way, and a great deal of this publicity penetration is wasted if an already publicized title is discarded.

This situation developed in connection with "Duel in the Sun." It was determined that other titles under consideration, such as "The Devil Saw Her First," had a higher acceptance rating. A publicity penetration survey, however, indicated that 10 per cent of the nation's moviegoers were already familiar with a movie called "Duel in the Sun," when the title change was considered. It was not thought economical, therefore, to lose that much audience penetration as a result of a title change.[2]

There are four different techniques which can be employed to determine the strength of a motion picture title:

(a) Absolute title tests
(b) Relative title tests
(c) Tests with control titles of unknown strength (pilot titles)
(d) Tests with control titles of an average acceptance rating

The relative title tests and the ones using an average control title are most widely used at the present time.

In *the absolute title test* an attempt is made to determine the drawing power of a title through the use of a "want-to-see" question. The results may be expressed in a percentage indicating the proportion of a cross-section which claimed that they are interested in seeing a picture purely on account of a certain

[2] Robert P. Brundage, "Dr. Gallup Polls Public So Hollywood Can Film the 'Perfect' Picture," *Wall Street Journal,* October 23, 1946.

title. For example, if two titles are under consideration for a picture, two such want-to-see questions are put before the respondents separately. The title receiving the greater amount of positive answers is the one with the greater drawing power.

This method makes it possible to establish an average rating of "zero" or 100. It could be assumed that a hypothetical "average" title would receive an equal number of positive and negative answers. In other words a title that leads 60 per cent of the moviegoers to say they would be interested in seeing a picture and 40 per cent not, could be rated as 100 plus 10, or 110. "No opinion" or "don't know" could either be eliminated or distributed in the same proportion as the other answers.

The advantage of this method is that the value of an individual title can be tested and it may be compared with previous tests of the same kind. The disadvantage is that almost all titles are likely to receive rather high ratings, and it is sometimes difficult to distinguish finely enough between the relative appeal of two or more apparently interesting titles.

Measured on an absolute basis an average title would register somewhat as follows:

Question: "If you knew nothing about a motion picture except that its title is "Manhattan Adventure" would you want to see it or not?"

Want to see it	59%
Do not want to see it	28
No opinion	13
Total	**100%**

Attention is drawn again to the high proportion of respondents who said they would see the picture merely on account of their interest in the title "Manhattan Adventure." This high want-to-see rating, which is largely due to the indiscriminating attitude of the nonselective movie audience, will be discussed later.

The *relative title test* method is more widely used than the one just described. This technique compares the strength of two or more titles weighted against each other. It is of value when a number of titles are under consideration with the object of finding out which one has the greatest pull.

The following table shows the detailed results of a title test of this type.[3] There were five titles under consideration:

A. Cargo of Innocence
B. His First Command
C. Full Speed Ahead
D. Stand By for Action
E. Come Hell or High Water

The results show that the title "Stand By for Action" was not only selected by almost half of the respondents but also that it led consistently in nineteen of the twenty locations where the interviews were conducted.

The percentages in Table 14 are based on approximately one hundred interviews in each location and approximately two

TABLE 14

BREAKDOWN ACCORDING TO LOCATION

	A	B	C	D	E	Total
Manhattan, N. Y.	14%	20%	6%	48%	12%	100%
Brooklyn, N. Y.	16	19	11	51	3	100
Bronx, N. Y.	11	18	14	51	6	100
Queens, N. Y.	11	13	19	53	4	100
Jersey City, N. J.	9	14	14	57	6	100
Bronxville Mt. Vernon, N. Y. Yonkers	12	14	15	53	6	100
Buffalo, N. Y.	9	22	15	49	5	100
Philadelphia, Pa.	35	21	6	27	11	100
Pittsburgh, Pa.	12	12	9	51	16	100
Boston, Mass.	11	26	16	40	7	100
Rochester, N. Y.	18	11	12	51	8	100
Los Angeles, Cal.	17	13	14	39	17	100
St. Louis, Mo.	9	15	14	57	5	100
Atlanta, Ga.	12	13	14	47	14	100
San Diego, Cal.	18	22	18	31	11	100
Cleveland, Ohio	16	24	4	53	3	100
Lawrence, Mass.	20	11	11	46	12	100
Providence, R. I.	11	14	10	53	12	100
Total	14%	16%	12%	49%	9%	100%

[3] The figures are published with the permission of Metro-Goldwyn-Mayer, for which the study was conducted in 1942.

thousand interviews for the "total" results. The interviews were in every instance controlled according to sex, age, and income groups. Only moviegoers were questioned.[4]

In tests of this sort the titles are generally printed on cards, on the assumption that most respondents will eventually be exposed visually to the final title. Provisions may be made to rotate the order in which the cards are presented to the interviewee.

In case there are more than three titles under consideration it may prove advantageous to narrow the choice of the best-liked title gradually. The respondent may be asked first to pick two titles from a list of four or five. After the choice is narrowed down to two titles, the respondent is asked which one of these two he likes better.

In the case of the aforementioned title test for the picture "Stand By for Action," the following technique was employed.

Question (1): If you were going to the movies and could see two of these five pictures, which two would you pick?

After the respondent selected two pictures he was asked the next question.

Question (2): If you were going tonight, which *one* picture of the two you picked would you rather see?

In this example the five titles under discussion were entirely different. The respondents had no reason to believe that they were dealing with titles of one and the same picture.

The advantage of the relative tests is that they register very clearly even slight differences in the drawing power of various titles. The variance in the indication of drawing power is demonstrated by the following figures. Two titles designated here as A and B were tested first independently (absolute method) and then comparatively (relative method).

While the relative method showed a difference of 60 per cent the absolute method showed a difference of only 20 per cent. It may be remarked here that of the two titles used for this ex-

[4] The leading title "Stand By for Action" was used finally for this Metro-Goldwyn-Mayer production, which starred Robert Taylor, Charles Laughton, and others.

periment, one had a very high drawing power and the other an unusually low acceptance rating.

	Absolute Technique (Two separate surveys)	*Relative Technique* (One survey)
Title "A"	56%	80%
Title "B"	36	20
		100%

One disadvantage of the relative method may be seen in the fact that the title value cannot be compared with that of other titles tested previously or later unless, for example, the leading title was or is again compared with another one under consideration. Also it may be possible that even the title which registers as best in a relative study is, absolutely speaking, not a very good one. It may have occurred that two or more unappealing titles were being examined. However, the relative tests meet business requirements quite satisfactorily in most cases, and give the answer to the all important question: Which of these titles would get more paying customers to the box-office?

Sometimes the problem arises of determining the different drawing power of titles, the nature of which would make it obvious or probable to the respondent that they are meant for the *same* picture. There are different ways of attempting to obtain reliable results in this case.

One method consists of conducting tests with *control titles of unknown strength.* Different surveys are made comprising identical samples, and the similar titles under the test are put between pilot titles. Let us assume it is necessary to determine whether "Ziegfeld Follies of 1946," or just "Ziegfeld Follies" is a better title for a motion picture. Following this method, it is necessary to make up two additional titles and conduct two surveys covering, for example, the following sets of titles:

First Set:	Music for All
	Ziegfeld Follies of 1946
	The Blue Phantom
Second Set:	Music for All
	Ziegfeld Follies
	The Blue Phantom

The better title is the one that registers highest in one of the two combinations.

In a test of this sort actually conducted, 'Ziegfeld Follies of 1946" received a higher rating than "Ziegfeld Follies." The apparent reason for this was that some of the respondents confused "Ziegfeld Follies" with previous productions that had a similar title, for instance "The Great Ziegfeld." The addition of "1946" made it clear to everybody that the picture in question was not a revival of an old production.

The *test with "average" control titles* is another method of determining the attractiveness of individual titles that has been used extensively by Audience Research, Inc. That organization has established a number of control titles which are never used on pictures or otherwise publicized. They register always "average," designated as 100, on a scale used by the institute.

Here is an actual result of six title tests conducted by Audience Research, Inc., for the RKO picture "Lady Luck" with the use of control titles.

The following titles were considered and tested for this picture, and received these ratings: [5]

> "D-Day in Las Vegas" 91
> "Lady's Choice" 100
> "The Lady's in Luck" 100
> "Lucky Lady" 106
> "The Lady Is Lucky" 117
> "Lady Luck" 118

According to Audience Research, Inc., the difference between the number of people found to be interested in seeing a picture entitled "D-Day in Las Vegas" and the number interested in seeing one entitled "Lady Luck" is six million admissions.[6]

Whenever title tests are conducted, regardless of which one of the methods mentioned before is being employed, an attempt is usually made to determine more than an over-all rating. The

[5] William R. Weaver, "Audience Research Answers the Question of 'What's in a Name?'" *Motion Picture Herald,* July 27, 1946.

[6] "Hitler's Children," incidentally, submitted simply as a title without supplemental information of any kind, registered 160, which is the all time high recorded by this institute.

reports include breakdowns indicating the variance of drawing power upon the different sections of the audience. This is especially important when the picture and title under analysis is supposed to appeal to a specific audience group, such as the younger moviegoers. By the same token it is possible to find out which sectors of the audience dislike a certain title. It is possible that a title sounds extremely attractive to men but is not liked very much by women. The high interest on the part of the men may result in a favorable over-all rating, but it is still possible that many of the female customers may be lost because they are not attracted by the title. A good title analysis provides, therefore, for sex, age, income, and other breakdowns.

TABLE 15

QUESTION: WHO WAS TENNESSEE JOHNSON?

	Men	Women	Total
President	33%	34%	33%
Vice-President under Lincoln	3	3	3
General	1	2	2
Statesman	2	...	1
Vice-President	1	...	1
Miscellaneous correct answers	2	1	1
Incorrect answers	1	1	1
Don't know	57	59	58
Total	100%	100%	100%

Another type of title test which may be conducted in conjunction with one of the types above is used to determine the audience comprehension or anticipation of the sort of motion picture suggested by a title. Usually motion picture producers try to give their audience an inkling, in the title, of the type of picture to be expected. There may be situations, however, in which they do not wish to do so. Some famous war pictures were released at a time when this type of picture was considered unpopular, and they bore somewhat misleading titles. Surveys can easily determine what moviegoers expect from a picture about which they know nothing except its title.

Before a picture called "Tennessee Johnson" was released, a special study was conducted to determine what the average moviegoer would expect to see. Table 15 shows the answers received through about seven hundred interviews conducted in ten different locations.

From the proportion of "don't know's" it is obvious that a large part of the audience would not know what to expect from a picture with this title.

AUDIENCE APPEAL AND COMPREHENSION
OF INDIVIDUAL SCENES AND HAPPENINGS

Every motion picture is seen by an extensive cross-section of the American people. It has to be witnessed by a great many persons to be profitable. The average picture is, therefore, produced with the intention of interesting and appealing to as

TABLE 16
QUESTION: WHO WAS ROBERT E. LEE?

	Men	Women	Total
Confederate General	52%	50%	51%
General in Civil War	13	14	13
General	14	10	12
In Civil War	1	3	2
Miscellaneous correct answers	1	2	2
Incorrect answers	8	6	7
Don't know	11	15	13
Total	100%	100%	100%

many different kinds of moviegoers as possible, not just a certain section of the audience; and one of the factors that might lessen its appeal is lack of understanding of some elements of the movie by part of the audience. These elements that mar the comprehension of the film may be single words, references, or entire scenes. Audience research can be used to discover the factors which cause difficulty so that they may be changed and expressed more clearly, or, if the producer so decides, eliminated.

For example, in one motion picture a reference to Robert E. Lee was considered. A survey among a representative sample of seven hundred moviegoers revealed the results in Table 16.

In the same manner it can be found out before or while the

picture is being produced whether certain jokes, punchlines, references to actual or fictional happenings, are comprehended by the average motion picture patron. Depending on the results of the survey, the lines or scenes under analysis may be changed.

So far there has been very little done in this field, even though it is probable that a highly specialized form of research might develop to assure an efficient and rapid handling of such problems. The choice of certain scenes in a motion picture, especially their emphasis and length as expressed in film footage, may some day be influenced by audience research.

The surveys to determine the relative audience preferences and dislikes for certain types of motion picture stories are one step in this direction. A picture is never a hundred per cent *western, mystery,* or *comedy.* It is predominantly a *western, mystery,* or *comedy,* but it usually includes many other basic story types. A *western* picture might, and often does, include elements such as mystery, comedy, romance, and so on, but just which blends in which proportions are most pleasing to the greatest number of people in the potential audience is still not known. It might evolve, for example, that a blend of romance is desirable in all kinds of pictures, but that people resent the introduction of, say, comedy in mystery stories.[7]

It is not inconceivable that the extent to which the different story elements should be blended to please the audience may be determined by research studies. The same would hold true for atmosphere and background. This very thought may horrify some producers and directors. But their approval will encourage this research and it is for their benefit that this type of specialized research would be conducted.

A tentative step in this direction may be seen in the following section on the subject of film analyzers.

POLYGRAPH RECORDERS

Film writers, directors, producers, and editors work for several months on all phases and details of a motion picture. They

[7] Marjorie Fiske and Leo Handel, Motion Picture Research, *The Journal of Marketing,* October, 1946.

witness scenes being shot and reshot, and look over parts of the picture in the studio projection rooms. It is difficult for men who have worked intensively on a picture to put themselves in the position of the average moviegoer who sees the film only once.

Two methods have been developed which enable the motion picture producer to discover before the picture is finally released how it will appear to the public and which parts of it are particularly liked or disliked. One of these methods, the analytical preview, will be discussed in a later chapter. The second method, the program analyzer or profile machine, will be treated here.

Most of the devices designed to measure audience reactions while the subjects are exposed to the medium are based on the original program analyzer conceived and designed for use in radio research by Paul F. Lazarsfeld of Columbia University and Frank Stanton of the Columbia Broadcasting System. An examination of the basic Lazarsfeld-Stanton program analyzer will make it easier to understand the other devices.

THE LAZARSFELD-STANTON PROGRAM ANALYZER[8]

The Lazarsfeld-Stanton program analyzer originally constructed to test radio programs is a device which enables a subject to record his reaction to a film as he watches it. The reactions are recorded in terms of Like, Dislike, or Indifference.

The viewer holds a green button in one hand and a red button in the other. If he likes a particular part of the motion picture, he presses the green button and keeps it pressed down for as long as his approval continues. If he dislikes what he sees and hears, he uses the red button in a similar fashion. If he feels indifferent, he does not press either button. The buttons are connected electrically to a battery of pens, resting on a continuously moving paper tape. When a button is pressed, the corresponding pen is jogged down an eighth of an inch perpendicular to the tape. The pen remains in this position until the button is re-

[8] See Lazarsfeld, Paul F., and Stanton, Frank, *Radio Research, 1942–43.*

leased. Timing pens serve to synchronize reactions with the program. The result is a continuous record, accurately timed, of the listener's feelings during each second of the broadcast, or the moviegoer's reaction to a motion picture.

Responses are thus caught at the time they are experienced, and possible errors in retrospective reporting of reactions are reduced to a minimum. The following steps are usually involved in testing a film in this way:

The content of the film is analyzed to determine the types of responses likely to be elicited. (This list of potentially significant elements also serves as an interview guide.)

The film is then shown to representative segments of the intended audience, in groups of ten since the program analyzer at present accommodates only this number, who record their immediate reactions.

Questionnaires are given to each subject before and after the film is seen. These questionnaires provide information about the respondent and serve as one measure of the educational or attitudinal effects of the film.

These steps are frequently accompanied by group interviews to determine the detailed nature of the subject's reaction. The interviews are recorded and the final analysis is then based on three sets of data: program analyzer's graphs, questionnaires, and transcripts of interviews.

The total number of Likes and Dislikes is usually presented graphically in the form of a profile. One such profile is shown in Chart 1. A time scale, in minutes, has been laid out across the chart. A legend at the bottom divides the film into sequences. A vertical scale runs along the left side of the chart showing the positive and negative reactions expressed in percentage based on the total number of viewers.[9]

It is thus possible to determine at a glance where the peaks and valleys of audience reactions are. The focused interviews following the film can then be directed to determine what about these scenes was particularly liked or disliked.

---

[9] The Army used a similar equipment for film evaluation studies, the Esterline-Angus, model A.W., portable recorder with 20 ink-writing polygraphic units.

CIRLIN REACTOGRAPH CHART

"GREEN DOLPHIN STREET" Produced by: CAREY WILSON Directed by: VICTOR SAVILLE

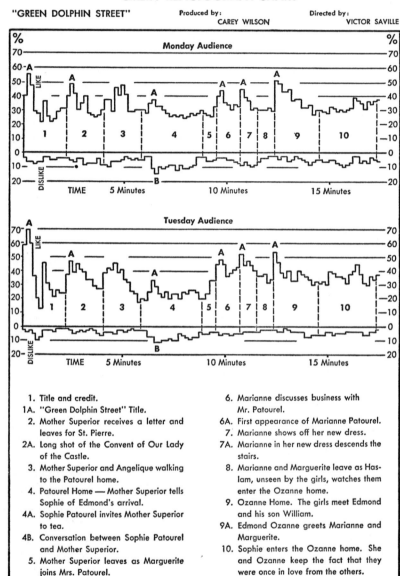

1. Title and credit.
1A. "Green Dolphin Street" Title.
2. Mother Superior receives a letter and leaves for St. Pierre.
2A. Long shot of the Convent of Our Lady of the Castle.
3. Mother Superior and Angelique walking to the Patourel home.
4. Patourel Home — Mother Superior tells Sophie of Edmond's arrival.
4A. Sophie Patourel invites Mother Superior to tea.
4B. Conversation between Sophie Patourel and Mother Superior.
5. Mother Superior leaves as Marguerite joins Mrs. Patourel.

6. Marianne discusses business with Mr. Patourel.
6A. First appearance of Marianne Patourel.
7. Marianne shows off her new dress.
7A. Marianne in her new dress descends the stairs.
8. Marianne and Marguerite leave as Haslam, unseen by the girls, watches them enter the Ozanne home.
9. Ozanne Home. The girls meet Edmond and his son William.
9A. Edmond Ozanne greets Marianne and Marguerite.
10. Sophie enters the Ozanne home. She and Ozanne keep the fact that they were once in love from the others.

Study Director — Bernard D. Cirlin
Associate — Jack N. Peterman

Report — R 108
April, 1947

CHART 1

THE CIRLIN REACTOGRAPH

Basically the Reactograph, as developed by Bernard D. Cirlin, is identical to the Lazarsfeld-Stanton program analyzer. Its technical development, however, differs from the original device.

The recorder unit of the Reactograph consists of a chemically treated moving tape against which rest fifty electrical styli. Two buttons are attached to each stylus by a pair of wires. As the respondents view a motion picture, they press the red button to express their dislike and the green button to express their approval. As they press the button an electrical current passes through the stylus and burns a mark into the chemically treated paper. If they press the Dislike button a dotted line appears on the paper, and if they press the Like button a solid line appears. If they have no reaction no mark is shown. Along the left hand margin of the tape the time intervals are marked so that it can be seen which individual has expressed approval or disapproval for every second of the motion picture.

The recorder unit can be attached to a totalizer. The totalizer shows in graphic form the total number of people expressing likes and dislikes for each two second interval. The test produces two detailed records. One is a chart showing a like and dislike profile; the other is the recorder tape which shows how each individual reacted during the picture.

In addition to getting a reaction graph for the total group, a subgroup totalizer may be used. This subgroup totalizer would produce separate like and dislike profiles for men and women, people of different age groups, or for any other breakdown of the audience that may be desired.

THE HOPKINS ELECTRIC TELEVOTING MACHINE

This device is used by Audience Research, Inc., in connection with its Preview Jury system. The picture is screened again before a representative audience. In addition to the basic breakdowns such as sex, age, and income, the test audience is divided into two predetermined groups representing the ratio which wants and which does not want to see the picture in question.

This ratio is determined in previous surveys using the title, the principal cast, and a bare outline of the story as a guide for the interviews.

Every previewer keeps a dial in his hand which enables him to record five degrees of response to the scenes as they pass in succession on the screen. The following dial positions are provided.

Like very much
Like
Neutral
Dull
Very dull

The reaction recording machine consists of a compactly built mechanism similar in appearance to a slightly oversized portable typewriter. The machine reels off a chart-line on a white tape about five inches wide, recording the mean average reaction of the assembled observers to each scene in the motion picture being tested.[10] The Hopkins device can compute the cumulative reaction of a hundred viewers at a time.

The previewers are given questionnaires to fill out before and after the preview. The answers to the questions furnish information amplifying the group information expressed in the profile curve produced by the Televoter.

THE SCHWERIN SYSTEM

The Schwerin method or "number cueing" method is related in principle to the preceding procedures of testing films while the screening is in progress. Schwerin, however, does not use any mechanical devices to obtain the "profile" of a picture. He relies on questionnaires filled in by the participants of the tests at certain intervals while the picture is being shown. Schwerin developed this technique in the testing of radio and television programs, and entered the motion picture field late in 1949. An evaluation of his method would therefore be premature at this

[10] Weaver, W. R., "Studios Use Audience Research to Learn What Pleases Customers," *Motion Picture Herald,* July 20, 1946.

time. It is discussed here to round out the descriptions of the various procedures.

A sample audience which numbers approximately four hundred is roughly pre-selected on the basis of income, education, sex, age, and occupation. At the theater, each person in the audience completes a series of questionnaires which contain information concerning his moviegoing habits, his general likes and dislikes by type of motion picture entertainment, and his specific attitude toward and familiarity with the type of picture being tested.

A test director indoctrinates the audience about the method of indicating reactions during the session. During the screening, large numbers are flashed on a separate screen at intervals as the picture is being run. These numbers are the respondent's "cues," and correspond to numbers printed on the questionnaire. Opposite each of these printed numbers are three boxes, labeled "good," "fair," or "poor" (or "interesting," "mildly interesting," or "not interesting," depending on the type of picture being tested). When a number is flashed, the respondent checks his reaction to that portion of the film which he has seen since the last number flashed.

After the picture has ended, the test director leads an audience discussion period. Members of the audience are invited to express their opinions on specific portions of the picture they have just seen, from whatever point of view they desire. These comments, which may range from criticisms of acting, casting, production values, direction, music, etc., to strong endorsements of those and other points, are put down in question form. If a lady says, "I thought Jane Smith was wonderful in the scene in the church," the question would read, "Did you like Jane Smith's performance in the scene in the church?" When a sufficient number of comments have been noted, the whole audience is asked to vote on them.

Schwerin then matches his sample to the universe. In the process, many of the questionnaires will be discarded to bring respondents into the proper ratio. The final sample will include

250 to 350 completed questionnaires, and will be a true sample of the particular universe being investigated by the test. The cued reactions of this matched sample are reduced to a profile of the whole audience's reaction to the picture.

TECHNICAL DIFFERENCES OF FILM ANALYZERS
AND THEIR CONSEQUENCES

As mentioned at the beginning of this chapter, all program analyzers are based on the original device invented by Paul Lazarsfeld and Frank Stanton. The Lazarsfeld-Stanton program analyzer's capacity is at present low, limited to ten persons. The individual reactions are not combined automatically but must be summed up in a time-consuming clerical operation. Cirlin and Audience Research, Inc., streamlined the basic device and made it more practical for the actual commercial use in the motion picture field.

The device used by Audience Research, Inc., differs in some aspects from the Lazarsfeld-Stanton and Cirlin analyzers. The latter permits the recording of the individual reactions of every respondent. This method makes it possible to determine the actual number of persons who express like or dislike at a given time, and also provides permanent individual records to be used as bases for interviewing later.

Since the device used by Audience Research, Inc., does not record the individual reactions, the interpretation of results is apt to be less clear. A plus 10 reaction, for example, may mean that only a few viewers expressed an opinion and liked the specific sequence of the picture; or it may be interpreted to indicate that all persons registered a reaction and that more liked than disliked the scene. Moreover, there is no guide provided for subsequent interviews with the individual respondents.

The Lazarsfeld-Stanton program analyzer and the Cirlin Reactograph all use a three-point reaction scale, while the dial of the Hopkins Televoting Machine provides five different positions. Tests conducted by the Office of Radio Research, Columbia University, and the United States Army all resulted in the adoption of a three-point scale even though a more detailed reaction scale would be theoretically more desirable because it would permit a more detailed analysis.

In an attempt to increase the reaction scale the Office of Radio Research conducted a special experiment with two groups of listeners of a radio program.[11] Group A, comprising forty subjects, was instructed to use a three-point scale of Like, Indifference, and Dislike, while the thirty-nine subjects of Group B were instructed to use a five-point scale with the additional judgments of Extreme Like and Extreme Dislike.

The results of this experiment are given in Chart 2 which shows a portion of the program profiles produced for Group A and B, with the Extreme Likes and Extreme Dislikes of Group B drawn separately. In general, the two curves follow each other closely, the rank correlation from program parts being .76. The use of the five-point scale tends to decrease somewhat the number of Indifference reactions.

But the confusions introduced into the test by the more complicated button operation required to register five possible reactions may interfere with listening. While there can be no doubt as to the desirability of a graded reaction, it is also important that the psychological nature of the listening situation should approximate as closely as possible the ease of listening at home.

A simplification of registering devices seems particularly important for the testing of motion pictures. A motion picture test takes a considerable amount of time in the first place, a fact that increases the desirability of a simple registering mechanism that can be operated almost automatically.

Also, movies require the visual attention of the audience. And it is important not to disrupt the concentration of the respondent by a device that might distract his eyes from the screen.

There is a further purely mechanical difference between the analyzer used by Audience Research, Inc., and the other devices. The release of the buttons of the program analyzer results in an automatic return to the neutral position. If, therefore, a re-

[11] Lazarsfeld, Paul F., and Stanton, Frank: *Radio Research, 1942–43* (New York: Duell, Sloan, and Pearce, 1944), p. 326.

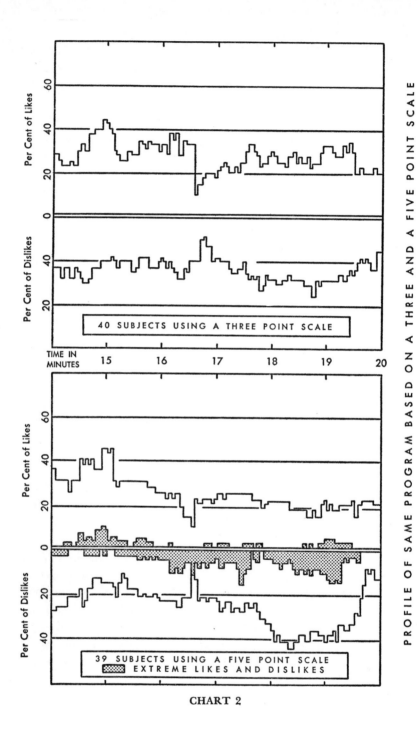

PROFILE OF SAME PROGRAM BASED ON A THREE AND A FIVE POINT SCALE

Per Cent of Likes

Per Cent of Dislikes

40 SUBJECTS USING A THREE POINT SCALE

TIME IN
MINUTES

Per Cent of Likes

Per Cent of Dislikes

39 SUBJECTS USING A FIVE POINT SCALE
EXTREME LIKES AND DISLIKES

CHART 2

spondent forgets to actuate the reaction mechanism he registers indifference. The dial used by Audience Research, Inc., does not revert automatically to neutral; and a respondent who forgets to indicate his reactions may have left the dial in a positive or negative position and in this manner distorts the results. In the case of the program analyzer, distortion would come about only when there is a question as to whether the respondent's interest is of a positive or negative nature.

ADVANTAGES AND LIMITATIONS OF THE MECHANICAL EDITORS

The major advantage of these devices is that they locate the sequence which gives rise to favorable or unfavorable responses more reliably than an interview alone, which has to depend on the respondent's recollection of what has caused his reaction. This enables a producer to study in detail important episodes of the picture evaluated by standards of judgment that closely approximate those of the average moviegoer. It makes it possible to determine audience reactions to a particularly crucial statement, the recognition of a subtle pun, the reception of an especially expensive set, or other such matters.

One of the most important difficulties lies in the different meanings which may be expressed in the subject's pressing buttons or turning a dial. Difficulties of interpretation will arise, for instance, when characters of the picture are intentionally designed to create a negative reaction from the viewer. This negative reaction to the "bad man" of the picture may register as a Dislike on the tape of a program analyzer, or "neutral" on the Televoting Machine, even though the interest in the sequence may be actually very high. This limitation may be overcome by intensive interviewing. The difficulty of interpreting correctly the meaning of Dislike reactions may also be reduced in advance by means of detailed instructions.

It is believed by some critics of these mechanical devices that members of test audiences may forget to actuate the apparatus when they become especially interested in the picture. Tests conducted by Bernard D. Cirlin and other experimenters, however, have shown that after a conditioning period of about three minutes the activation of the like and dislike buttons as used for the Lazarsfeld-Stanton analyzer and the Cirlin Reactograph is done unconsciously and automatically. The subject's actions may be compared to those of the driver of an automobile where the application of the brakes or gearshifting is done without a conscious effort.[12]

Some people, in fact, do not recall having pressed the buttons. One such incident was revealed when, following the test screening of "Green Dolphin Street," one elderly lady stated how very much she was impressed by an earthquake scene. She claimed she was so excited by this sequence that she forgot to push the Like button. But a reference to the recording tape revealed that she had pressed the Like button during the entire sequence with only a few interruptions.

RELIABILITY AND VALIDITY

There are two basic criteria by which the worth of any measuring instrument can be determined—reliability and validity. Knowing the reliability of the measuring device enables its user to know to what extent the results are consistent. Validity shows whether the device is measuring what it purports to measure.

One type of validity test was made in conjunction with "Green Dolphin Street" by setting up two test groups of moviegoers consisting of fifty persons. The profiles obtained by the two identical tests are presented in Chart 1.[13] The film analyzer used for this test was the Cirlin Reactograph. The results show that the two audience groups which were matched according to their sex, age, and socio-economic brackets produced almost identical profiles. The same major peaks for likes and dislikes occur in both charts. Such differences as do exist relate to minor ups and downs in the accumulated curves.

The technique of testing the same program on different lis-

[12] In order to give the audience the opportunity of familiarizing and conditioning itself to this research procedure, it has become a practice in the testing of pictures to show a short subject before screening the picture under examination.

[13] See page 48.

tener groups can also serve to indicate what size of sample is needed to produce a stable program profile. Table 17 shows the correlation obtained for a variety radio program between the total group of subjects and each of several smaller matched samples of this total group, according to the rank order of the scores for the different parts of the program. The table shows how the correlation increases with the size of the sample.

TABLE 17

VARIETY (RADIO) PROGRAM

Sample Size	Correlation
15	.64
25	.90
40	.92
55	.92
65	.98

It appears from this table that fairly small samples can be used to determine the relative popularity of the different parts of a radio program or motion picture. While these small samples would suffice to determine the probable trend of reactions and the general appeal of major sections of a program, they would not be sufficient to study the relative appeal of relatively small sections within the major sections themselves. The size of the sample, therefore, should depend upon the detail with which one wishes to measure a program.

Validity may be determined by comparing the results of the measuring device with results obtained by different methods of established validity. By comparing the evaluation of a program by the listener, as expressed on a questionnaire, to the second-by-second record of the program analyzer, it is possible to determine to some extent the validity of these second-by-second responses.

Such a comparison is given in Table 18, which shows the average score recorded on the program analyzer for the program as a whole, according to how the questions on liking the program were answered after the test. The table shows that people who on the questionnaire rated the program as "very interesting," the production and the content as "among the best" they had heard on the radio, and who said they would "listen again" if they happened to turn on the program, have a better score on the program analyzer than those who rated the production and content as "bad," the program itself as "boring," and who said they would have "turned it off" at home.

The average attitude score is determined from the Likes, Dislikes, and the Indifference reactions according to a method devised by Lazarsfeld and Robinson. The final score, called a

TABLE 18

AVERAGE ATTITUDE SCORE ON PROGRAM ANALYZER
ACCORDING TO PROGRAM EVALUATION BY MEANS OF
QUESTIONNAIRE

Questionnaire rating	Average program analyzer score
Program as a whole:	
Very interested	1.28
Interested	.85
Indifferent	.67
Bored	—.07
Production:	
One of the best	1.23
Very good	.83
Average	.76
Bad	—.50
Content:	
One of the best	1.12
Very good	1.12
Average	.57
Bad	—.07
If I happened to turn on this program:	
I would listen again	1.21
I would listen to end	.79
I would turn it off	.10

"trichometric" score, ranges from 0 to 3.19. The zero score represents complete indifference or an equal number of Likes and Dislikes. The 3.19 rating, if negative, signifies complete Dislike reaction throughout the entire broadcast; if positive, complete Like is indicated. A score, therefore, ranges between plus and minus 3.19.[14]

To date, the analyzer has been used largely to test the effectiveness of propaganda or educational films. In a test of educational films, it was found that the program analyzer is a

[14] Lazarsfeld, P. F., and Robinson, W. S., "Some Properties of the Trichotomy 'Like, No Opinion, Dislike' and Their Psychological Interpretation," *Sociometry*, Vol. III (1940), No. 2, 151–78.

surprisingly sensitive instrument for registering audience response and for eliciting the recall of part-by-part responses in interviewing.[15] The practical value of such tests is illustrated by their findings: auditory stimuli are incidental to visual stimuli in effect; responses easily change from like to dislike if a sequence lasts too long; transitions are usually met with indifference, as is very familiar material. They also found marked variations with sex and educational level.

Commercially the program analyzer has been most extensively used to test like and dislike of commercial radio programs, but it has similar possibilities for commercial films. Before the film goes into final production, certain scenes the directors are not sure of could be pretested to determine which version is better liked. If there is any doubt about which actor is better suited for a certain kind of role, this could be pretested also by shooting a few strategic scenes in advance, a procedure which would probably be especially useful in pretesting the appeal of a new actor.

But the most practical data, from the standpoint of commercial motion picture production, would be derived from a series of studies of various kinds of pictures among a sufficiently large segment of the population to determine general likes and dislikes among different age, sex, and socio-economic groups. Several questions could be answered in this way: there are some people who only go to see certain kinds of pictures. What do they like about these pictures? What do they dislike about other kinds of pictures? Are there ways of changing westerns, comedies, war pictures and so on so that more people would attend them? By showing a few representative pictures of various kinds to groups of non-moviegoers, it would be possible to find out what, specifically, they object to in motion pictures; and using a particular film as a starting point, it would then be possible to find out whether certain changes (e.g., the introduction of more realism) would convert any of these non-moviegoers.

Such general information about the effects of various kinds

[15] Sturmthal, A., and Curtis, A., "Program Analyzer Tests of Two Educational Films," *Radio Research, 1942–43.*

of motion pictures and the general preferences of several groups of the population would conceivably provide data for writers, directors, and producers which would enable them to give the motion picture public what it wants most. More significantly, such information would enable these leaders in the industry who are concerned with the production of more realistic and socially challenging feature films to determine to what extent pictures can be "upgraded" without losing a sizable portion of the audience as a consequence. It might then develop that such upgrading would bring into the ranks of regular moviegoers many people who now rarely or never attend.

CHAPTER *5* *Tests after the production*

Analytical previews are the research version of Hollywood sneak previews. They are undertaken after the picture is completed, by screening either an uncut version or the final release print. There are several reasons for conducting analytical previews.

If an uncut version is presented, the findings of the preview survey may be utilized in the final editions of the film. It is possible to get detailed information about the preview audience's response to the performance of the stars and of the players in the supporting cast. And information as to the best and the least liked sequences and happenings in the picture can also be ascertained.

If a final version is presented, an over-all audience rating may be obtained as a guide to the amount of advertising advisable, and certain well liked features of the movie may be discovered for use in promotional schemes.

There are two different methods of conducting analytical previews. One is the personal interview, the other the mail questionnaire approach. Each method has its merits and disadvantages which will be briefly summarized later. But first a brief description of the two methods.

For the purpose of an analytical preview followed by *personal interviews,* a picture is shown before its general release in one or more theaters which are found to have a fairly well diversified patronage. After the screening of the test picture, interviewers are stationed in the lobby of the theater to question the people who saw the picture. Usually it is necessary to employ from fifteen to twenty such interviewers to reach a sufficient number of respondents. The sample obtained in this manner covers, as a rule, 300 to 350 persons and is usually controlled by sex and age. As a rule, about two hours are available for the interviewing, since the previewed picture is followed by news, coming-attraction trailers, and perhaps one or two features. It has proven advantageous to have the interviewers work in teams of two. The majority of moviegoers attend in pairs, and if both persons are interviewed by two interviewers at the same time it eliminates, first of all, interference from the co-attendant. Secondly, each respondent is apt to pay more attention to his answers if he is not irritated by the fact that he is keeping another person waiting.

Tables 19 and 20 are taken from a report on a preview survey which was conducted for a Metro-Goldwyn-Mayer production, "Journey for Margaret." About 350 persons were interviewed after they had seen a preview of this picture at a theater in New York City in October, 1942.

TABLE 19

QUESTION: WHAT DO YOU THINK ABOUT THE PICTURE AS A WHOLE?

	Men	Women	Total
Excellent	21%	46%	34%
Very good, like it very much	59	45	51
Good, like it	9	5	7
Fair, pretty good	7	2	4
Didn't like it much, not good	1	...	1
Did not like it, bad	1	1	1
Dislike it very much, very bad	1	...	1
Propaganda	1	1	1
Total	100%	100%	100%

TABLE 20

QUESTION: WHAT DO YOU THINK ABOUT LARAINE DAY AS NORA DAVIS?

	Men	Women	Total
Excellent	31%	45%	38%
Very good (looking), like her very much	49	37	43
Good (looking), like her	4	9	7
Fair, pretty good	11	6	8
Didn't like her much, not good	3	1	2
Did not like her, bad	1	1	1
Other	1	1	1
Total	100%	100%	100%

Evaluation studies were also carried out by the U. S. Army to determine the audience appeal of some of the orientation films produced for the men in the armed forces. The following answer categories were used, and distribution of responses was obtained after the film "The Battle of Britain" was shown to a cross-section of army men. The question pertaining to evaluation ran as follows:

"If you saw one of the camp movies mentioned above, did you like it?" [1]

Yes, very much	77%
Yes, fairly well	16
No, not very much	4
No, not at all	2
No answer	1
Total	100%

The distribution of responses as shown for "Journey for Margaret" and "The Battle of Britain" gains in value whenever it is possible to use the same questioning procedure on comparable audiences for different pictures. The variations of answers will then indicate various degrees of preferences, audience appeal, interest, whatever the experimenter may have set out to measure.

Another question typical of preview surveys is the following which was put to 525 respondents after they saw a preview of the picture "Tennessee Johnson."

[1] Hovland, C. I., Lumsdaine, A. A., and Sheffield, F. D., *Experiments on Mass Communications* (Princeton, N. J.: Princeton University Press, 1949), p. 86.

TABLE 21

QUESTION: IF A FRIEND OF YOURS ASKED YOU WHETHER OR NOT TO
SEE THIS PICTURE, WHAT WOULD YOU SAY?

	Men	Women	Total
See it	91%	93%	92%
Not see it	1	1	1
Other answers	8	6	7
Total	100%	100%	100%

Questionnaires used for preview surveys also contain other questions such as:

Which actors in the supporting cast did you like best?
Which actors in the supporting cast did you not like?
Which scenes or episodes did you particularly like?
Which scenes or happenings if any, did you not like?
Were there any scenes which you thought too lengthy?

The reactions of the audience obtained in this manner are especially significant if they are compared with the results of surveys covering other motion pictures.

The mail questionnaire method is in principle very similar to the personal interview approach. Instead of being interviewed, the preview patrons are handed questionnaires with the request to take them home, fill them in within a few days, and mail them back to the research office. The underlying purpose of this technique is to have some time elapse between the respondent's exposure to the picture and his expression of appreciation or criticism.

This method provides for answers to specific questions and, therefore, draws specific reactions and permits an intelligent detailed tabulation. Also it indicates the classification data (age, sex, occupation, etc.) of the respondent and in this manner makes it possible to determine whether or not a representative sample has been obtained.

The following figures indicate the returns from a typical preview mail questionnaire. An advance screening of the Metro-Goldwyn-Mayer picture entitled, "The Mighty McGurk" was held in New York in 1946. Following the screening, 950 preview questionnaires were distributed among the audience. The forms could be folded and sealed so that they resembled business reply envelopes, with the postage to be collected from the addressee. An attempt was made to distribute them evenly among men and women, and to favor the "under thirty" age group. One hundred sixty-eight or 17.7 per cent of the questionnaires were mailed to the research office within a week. A few straggler ballots followed later but could not be used for the analysis. All but five of the questionnaires were filled in well enough for tabulating. Seventy-nine per cent of the respondents answered all questions, the others did not fill in answers to the open-ended questions (Which scenes did you enjoy most?). Of the 163 questionnaires used for tabulation, 48 per cent were filled in by male respondents, 52 per cent by women; 66 per cent by persons under thirty years of age and 34 per cent by persons over thirty years. This rate of return can be considered about average for a motion picture audience sample.

An advantage of the interview method is, first of all, that it is possible to control the sample by a selection from the audience. Secondly, all questionnaires are filled in completely and correctly by professional interviewers. The results of the survey, moreover, are available a few hours after the questioning is terminated.

This method has one main drawback. It is evident from the results of such surveys that many moviegoers will be inclined to talk favorably about a motion picture if asked to evaluate it immediately after the exposure. They lack the necessary time perspective to judge it properly, and there is the added possibility that they will give answers which they think will please the interviewers.

For the purpose of comparing one picture with another, this inflation of favorable reactions is not as harmful as might be expected. The figures are still relatively comparable, since the scores of all pictures are conditioned in the same fashion.

It was an attempt to reduce the number of spurious favorable replies which led to experiments with the mail questionnaire.

The questionnaire permits the respondents to gain a better judgment after "sleeping over the picture," and to compare it, knowingly or not, with other pictures they have seen, or with the cumulative impressions of those pictures. Most of these preview questionnaires are filled in one or two days after the picture has been seen and, consequently, the over-all ratings are usually lower than those obtained through coincidental interviews.

The drawback of the mail questionnaire method lies in the difficulty of controlling the size and composition of the sample in as satisfactory a manner as when personal interviews are conducted in the theater. This method is also slower, as it is necessary to wait at least a week until the bulk of the questionnaires are returned to conclude the tabulation. Such a delay may be too great for the motion picture time table. Also it has been observed that some questions, especially the open-answer ones, frequently are not filled in.

Here, too, we meet the problem that better-educated persons are more apt to fill in the questionnaires, and that persons who liked the picture are also more likely to return the ballot than those who did not care for it.

There is one way to overcome the main weaknesses of both the interviewing and mail questionnaire method. This is to obtain the names, addresses, and classification data of persons who attended the preview and conduct the actual interview one or two days later at the home of the respondent. This is a rather costly and slow method but the results are superior to either of the other techniques.

Another method in sneak preview handling has been suggested by George Sidney, Metro-Goldwyn-Mayer director, who has been concerned with the possibility that sneak previews, as presently conducted, have outlived their usefulness because of the "professional" critics who seek out the supposedly unannounced showings and then fill out comment cards.

Use of the applause and laugh meter has already proved its worth in pictures where a spontaneous result is possible, according to Sidney, but new equipment and techniques will make it possible to get honest reactions to serious dramatic situations in which tenseness, rather than any overt reaction, is supposed to result. One method now in the experimental stage involves the photographing of the audience from a concealed camera using infra-red film. The audience does not know the photograph has been made, and since it is timed to a particular second, the director and producer can get a true picture of the audience's interest.

Another technique being tested is the use of concealed microphones to pick up conversations as the audience leaves the theater after the preview. In one such test six concealed mikes were used, and due to the slow flow of the audience from the auditorium and lobby, it was possible to pick up uninhibited reactions to the picture.

Still another device along these lines has been reported under consideration[2] by Loren L. Ryder. The head of Paramount Studio's sound department is developing a small electronic gadget to record the spectator's heartbeat and rate of breathing as scenes of love, violence, and excitement unfold upon the screen. The instrument is designed to be placed under a certain number of seats in the theater.

Indications are that tests made after the completion of a motion picture are losing out in favor of surveys which can be carefully conducted at a time when adjustments in the picture can still be made. These tests were described in Chapter 3. Preview surveys conducted with the aid of mail questionnaires or personal interviews are, however, important to establish the enjoyment level of a motion picture. This application has led to the establishment of an "audience appeal index" which was introduced by the Motion Picture Research Bureau, and is described in detail in the following section.

THE AUDIENCE APPEAL INDEX

The degree of public acceptance of a radio program or a newspaper can be established in a purely quantitative manner. The radio producer asks: "How many persons listen to my pro-

[2] *Hollywood Reporter,* December 4, 1946.

gram?" This proportion can be determined through sampling methods and expressed in a rating, such as supplied by Hooper, Nielsen, and the Broadcasting Measurement Bureau. A newspaper publisher checks his circulation figures and can determine exactly how many persons buy, and estimate approximately how many persons read his publication. Continuous checks on newspaper circulation or program listenership make it possible to measure an increase or decrease in the audience, which indicates changes in the public acceptance of the medium.

A quantitative measurement of the public acceptance rate of a motion picture is the compilation of box-office returns.[3] But other influences, such as a vigorous promotional campaign, may result in box-office returns higher than the standard of the picture itself would justify. The audience appeal index aims to express the audience *evaluation* of a picture rather than merely its acceptance. It embodies a new approach and, therefore, is subject to improvement in some respects.

The audience appeal index has two principal functions. As mentioned above, it expresses the quality of a picture as seen by the average audience in the form of a rating. Second, and of greater interest to the industry, is the fact that the audience appeal index makes it possible in some degree to measure, anticipate, and exploit word-of-mouth advertising.

The audience appeal level of a picture can be determined as soon as the final print is ready for exhibition. Three to four analytical previews are conducted in different locations to obtain the reaction of a cross-section of moviegoers. The sample should be well stratified according to sex, age, and social levels.

The index is based on the answers to a key question such as: "If somebody asked you about the picture, how would you grade it?" Or "What do you think about the picture as a whole?"

To help the respondent in grading the picture, and to receive answers which can be used for tabulation, a checklist is used which provides, for example, the following categories: *excellent, very good, good, fair, not so good, bad, very bad.* Two sets

[3] See Chapter 1.

of checklists are used, showing the evaluations in different order.

The appeal values correspond to ratings ranging, for example, from 100 for excellent to zero for very bad. The same appeal values and corresponding ratings have to be used in every instance to obtain a true basis for comparison.

The audience appeal index is finally established by adding the appeal ratings obtained and dividing them by the number of respondents covered by the survey.

THE APPEAL INDEX AND WORD-OF-MOUTH ADVERTISING

Word-of-mouth advertising is one of the most potent influences on movie attendance. Its importance can be recognized by the following table. A survey conducted by the Motion Picture Research Bureau in 1943 indicated that among all sources of information about a picture, personal recommendation ranks as the most influential.

TABLE 22

THE RELATIVE IMPORTANCE OF THE DIFFERENT SOURCES FROM WHICH THE
ATTENDANTS LEARNED ABOUT THE PICTURE

	Men	Women	Total
Reviews, articles in newspapers	16%	12%	14%
Movie page on day of movie visit	5	4	4
Ads in papers before attendance day	11	8	10
Signs on theater	3	3	3
Preview trailer	16	13	15
Movie magazines	1	4	2
National magazines	1	1	1
Hearsay	28	36	32
Radio	3	3	3
Posters and billboards	1	1	1
Ads in or on other theaters	1	1	1
Other	2	2	2
None	12	12	12
Total	100%	100%	100%

The audience appeal index makes it possible to exploit word-of-mouth advertising in the following manner:

Pictures with a high audience appeal can be marketed slowly, and not rushed into general release, in order to give word-of-mouth advertising ample time to develop and to draw large audiences.

Pictures with a low audience appeal, on the other hand, can be released as fast as possible in the subsequent runs to take fullest advantage of the company-controlled advertising and publicity, and to get as little interference as possible from unfavorable word-of-mouth publicity.

THE ANTICIPATED PICTURE APPEAL

Another phenomenon of motion picture marketing about which we have only a limited knowledge may be mentioned briefly in this context. There is an interdependence between the audience appeal of a picture and the moviegoer's expectancy level of entertainment. These two elements are tied up in turn with company-controlled advertising and publicity, and word-of-mouth propaganda. The correlation of these factors doubtless has a bearing on box-office revenues and, therefore, on the number of theater admissions per advertising dollar.

The expectancy level of entertainment is a term describing the moviegoer's degree of anticipated enjoyment of the motion picture (stage play, radio show, etc.) he is planning to see. This expectancy level may have been contrived in the subject's mind by considering the stars, title, and story type, but more often it will also be affected by advertising, professional critics, and word-of-mouth publicity.

The interrelation of the expectancy level and audience appeal of a picture is a familiar criterion with every moviegoer. A movie visit may be undertaken with the anticipation of seeing an outstanding picture. If the film in question is one of an average audience appeal, however, the discrepancy between the high expectation and the moderate enjoyment may result in disappointment and, possibly, dislike of the picture. Had the same moviegoer been under the impression that the picture he was about to see was not very good he might have enjoyed it considerably, due to the fact that the picture appeal was higher than the anticipated enjoyment.

The reactions of the moviegoer may find expression, moreover, in successive favorable or unfavorable word-of-mouth publicity, depending on the relation between audience appeal and expectancy level of enjoyment. The interrelation of these factors may be presented schematically as follows:

Expectancy level of enjoyment	Appeal of picture	Actual enjoyment	Resulting word-of-mouth publicity
High	Average	Low	Negative
Low	Average	High	Positive

The motion picture industry has demonstrated a growing interest in this line of reasoning. Whenever possible, only pictures which have proved to be of above average audience appeal are supported by powerful promotional campaigns. A picture must, so to speak, deserve its advertising. Experience has shown that high-powered selling campaigns may boomerang if the product does not warrant them, due to the discrepancy between anticipated and actual audience appeal.

Some evaluation studies concern themselves with criteria other than the audience appeal. Educational pictures, for example, aim to impart information rather than to provide amusement. It may be assumed that an entertaining film will be a better teaching device than a dull film even though it is conceivable that in some instances the entertainment value of a picture may interfere somewhat with the educational objective. The picture "The Battle of Britain" was subject to evaluations from various points of view. For example, to get the soldiers' opinion of the truthfulness of the presentation the following question was asked and the following answers were obtained: [4]

Did you think "The Battle of Britain" gave a fair and accurate picture of the events?

"Yes, it gave a true picture of what was happening"	65%
"It was true in most respects but it seemed to give a onesided view at times"	33
"No, it did not give a really true and honest picture of the facts"	2
Total	100%

[4] Experiments on Mass Communications, p. 87.

It was found that an audience that regards a film as "propaganda" will, most likely, be more resistant to its influence, especially the members of the audience who were initially predisposed against the propagandistic message of the film. To determine whether "The Battle of Britain" was considered propaganda by the soldiers, the experiment included the question "What do you think was the reason for showing this movie to you and to the other men?" Most of the men felt that the purpose of the screenings was to familiarize them with the facts of war. About one-fourth of the answers suggested that the film aimed to manipulate the attitude and motives of the men; only a negligible proportion of the men used the word "propaganda." It became evident, therefore, that "The Battle of Britain" was not regarded a propaganda film by the great majority of the soldier audience. Among the relatively small number of the men who considered the film propagandistic, two principal interpretations of "propaganda" were discernible, one pertaining to distortion of facts and the other to manipulative purpose of the showing of the films regardless of whether the material presented was true or distorted.

Another complex of studies conducted after the production of a picture concerns itself with the effect of films on its audience. Due to the various ramifications of this type of research, Chapter 12 is devoted to the effect of movies.

REVIVAL STUDIES

Revivals of productions of former years on a national scale became quite frequent during the recent war. After the hostilities ended and a shortage of products developed, an ever-increasing number of distributors saw their chance to fill gaps in exhibition schedules with re-issues. And indications are that the motion picture industry will continue the process in the future. Pictures have reached a high degree of technical perfection, and many top productions which have been turned out within the last ten years have greater audience appeal than a second- or third-rate picture produced today. It can even be expected that this trend will become more important as time goes on.

The beginning of this trend may be seen in the case of "Gone with the Wind." To date this production has been released nationally four times. Provided that good prints remain available, and there is no reason why they should not, it may be re-released for many years to come.

The potential audience of a motion picture to be re-issued can be divided into two groups. First, persons who have seen the picture before and who are willing to see it again. And second, moviegoers who have not seen the picture before and want to see it as a revival. Important in the second group are persons who were not part of the potential audience during the original release of the picture. For example, there are persons who were too young at the time of the original release, or, of special importance at this time, men of the armed forces who were overseas for a long time and missed out on some productions.

By means of research studies, it is possible to measure the size of the market for pictures under consideration for a re-issue. A number of specific studies have been made to obtain an idea of the chance of a successful revival for certain pictures.

The Motion Picture Research Bureau conducted a general study of revivals in the summer of 1942. The survey was conducted among five hundred typical moviegoers in New York City and revealed that there is considerable interest in the presentation of the outstanding productions of the last ten years.

Here are some of the results of the study:

91 per cent of the respondents stated that they would like to see the outstanding pictures of the last ten years again.

8 per cent would not attend.

1 per cent had no opinion on the subject.

97 per cent of all respondents claimed they were willing to see old motion pictures they had not already seen. They would not be prejudiced by the fact that these pictures were produced in previous years.

90 per cent of the respondents were willing both to see old pictures again, and to see top productions they had not already viewed.

These percentages do not remain as high if respondents are narrowed down to specific motion pictures, but in any case they indicate a marked general interest in revivals.

CHAPTER 6 *Advertising and publicity research*

It is estimated that the motion picture industry spent 55.5 million dollars for advertising in the United States in 1948.[1] About 73 per cent of the expenditures were used for advertising in newspapers, 21 per cent for radio and 4 per cent for magazine advertising. The seven major companies spent about 20.5 million dollars for advertising space and radio time in 1948. The number of ads placed daily in the various media in the United States is estimated at 15,700 insertions.

Investigations pertaining to the promotion of motion pictures represent one of the most highly developed branches of film audience research, despite the relative complexity of the problems involved. This may be partly due to the fact that research finds a more widespread utilization among advertisers in general. Also, persons concerned with the selling and promoting of motion pictures would seem to be more receptive to the idea of research than those associated with production.

THE ADVERTISING PROBLEM OF THE MOTION PICTURE INDUSTRY

The advertising problem of the motion picture industry differs considerably from that of other types of enterprises. The

[1] *Film Daily Year Book of Motion Pictures,* 1949.

managements of most commercial organizations market products or services which are being offered and sold to the public over a considerable period of time, such as cigarettes, toilet articles, canned foods, automobiles, department store goods, beverages, transportation, etc. The advertising of all these has a common factor. It primarily promotes a name or a trademark which is constant. The advertisement, whether it is selling chewing gum or a luxury car, usually displays the trademark more prominently than any other information about the product.

For example:

CADILLAC
A Wiser Choice Than Ever

The trademark and slogan are prominently displayed, while details about the new car are shown in much smaller type below this heading.

The motion picture industry is the only important advertiser who does not and cannot base sales promotion on the trademark. Advertisements such as:

METRO-GOLDWYN-MAYER
presents
"The Next Voice You Hear"

which would be the counterpart of the above Cadillac advertisement, would be of little avail. The reason for this different advertising policy stems from the necessity of selling every motion picture independently. A partial exception to this rule may be seen in the release of a picture series such as the "Andy Hardy" or "Blondie" pictures. But even in this case it is the basic story type and cast, rather than the name of the producing company, on which promotional campaigns are based.

The potential audience is not at all interested in the producing company. As indicated in another chapter, moviegoers are primarily concerned with the cast and story. Only in comparatively rare instances are they aware of the producer and director (Selznick, Hitchcock).

Despite the fact that the average moviegoer is quite uninterested in the producing company and that the trademark is consequently not an important advertising element, the public is quite familiar with the trademarks of the leading motion picture firms. This was revealed by studies conducted by the Motion Picture Research Bureau which aimed to determine the relative popularity of the film trademarks.

A survey conducted in 1946 covered the leading firms. Over one thousand movie-patrons were questioned in fourteen selected locations. They were shown reproductions of the trademarks on which the names of the companies they represented were blocked out. Table 23 indicates the proportion of interviewers who were able to identify the trademarks.[2]

TABLE 23

TRADEMARK IDENTIFICATION

	Men	Women	Total
Columbia Pictures	24%	15%	19%
Metro-Goldwyn-Mayer	76	72	74
Monogram Pictures	32	17	25
Paramount Pictures	61	51	56
RKO Radio Pictures	28	14	21
Universal Pictures	23	14	19
Warner Brothers	7	5	6

Table 23 indicates also that men are more trademark conscious than women, even though we find women better informed in most other matters concerning motion pictures.

There is another factor which distinguishes motion picture advertising from other types. The major motion picture distributors release twenty-five to fifty pictures a year. This means that the movie advertisers may have to conceive, plan, carry out, and supervise a great number of entirely different campaigns at the same time. Referring again to our comparison with Cadillac cars, the comparable situation would be for this advertising department to promote thirty to fifty entirely different cars a year without taking advantage of the basic value of the trademark, "Cadillac." Advertising for the large majority of products has a

[2] Twentieth Century-Fox was not included in the survey because the name of the firm is an integral part of the trademark.

generating and preserving effect. Motion picture advertising, however, is concerned with the generating effect only.

Furthermore, a motion picture has to be sold to the public in a comparatively brief space of time, usually within the short period between the completion of the studio negative and the beginning of the national release. A high audience penetration must be achieved within a few months. Motion picture advertising has to create interest for a picture before its opening. A successful opening, in turn, can influence the entire career of a picture. Exhibitors all over the country who learn that a picture is well received at its first engagements will be more interested in renting it, and may schedule its showing on preferred playing days.

As soon as a studio accepts, or considers accepting, a story for a motion picture, publicity items begin to appear. There are no rules as to the manner in which such publicity is disseminated. It may be different for every picture. Organized advertising campaigns are set into motion as soon as the approximate date of the opening of the picture is determined. They generally begin with stories and advertisements in fan magazines, which are followed by advertisements in national magazines, and, finally, in local newspapers, along with radio commercials over local radio stations.

The advertising budget for many "A" pictures of the major distributors ranges from $100,000 to $200,000. Some pictures are supported by more substantial campaigns, costing millions of dollars.[3]

Advertising expenditures are usually divided between the national advertising efforts (national magazines, radio hookups, etc.) which are paid solely by the distributor, and co-operative local advertising comprising promotional expenditures which are paid partly by the local theater and partly by the distributor.

The industry tests the drawing power of campaigns by employing different approaches in test cities where the new picture is exhibited. An attempt is made to gauge the relative value of

[3] According to a report the advertising budget for "Duel in the Sun" amounted to nearly $2,000,000. See *New York Times*, December 21, 1947.

various campaigns from the differences in box-office revenues. This method entails considerable shortcomings, for factors such as the competitive situation, the drawing power of the co-feature, and the weather may influence the box-office takes more than the different campaigns under examination.

Research has emphasized that the advertising dollar is more effective if sales promotion is given time to develop. It is attempted, therefore, to plan as far ahead as possible to avoid cramming press campaigns into too brief a span of time. The total number exposed is also increased with a greater variety of outlets for advertising, publicity, and exploitation.

To sum it up, the significant features of motion picture advertising are (1) the necessity of promoting every picture separately because the trademark is of insignificant importance in motion picture advertising; (2) the necessity of carrying out campaigns for a number of different pictures at the same time; and (3) the speedy planning and executing of advertising campaigns.

The advertising chief of a major company may have to supervise simultaneously ten to fifteen pictures. It is of great importance to him to know to what degree the potential audiences for the different pictures have been successfully exposed to the various media of promotion. He is interested in getting a clear picture as to how his campaigns influence both his national and local audiences, and to see exactly how the dollars spent for advertising actually succeed in bringing customers to the box-office.

THE PUBLICITY AND POTENTIAL AUDIENCE INDEXES

Before World War II, both the Motion Picture Research Bureau and Audience Research, Inc., developed techniques to measure the degree of advertising and publicity penetration of a motion picture. The results may be expressed by indexes which show the proportion of moviegoers within a certain "population" who have read or heard about a film.

While the proportion of moviegoers who "know about" a certain picture is important, it is of even greater value to ascertain the proportion who were not only exposed to the various promotion media, but who also "want to see" the picture. Another index must be used, therefore, to indicate the part of the moviegoing public in which the desire to see a picture was created.

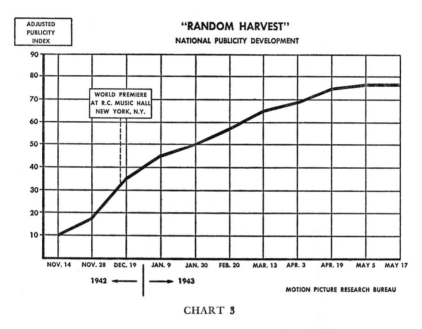

CHART 3

In their practical application, publicity development studies may be divided into long-range national studies and short-range local studies. The long-range national studies aim to report the results of the national promotional activities for a picture. They are usually conducted in certain key locations, beginning at the time controlled publicity begins and terminating when the picture has been released all over the nation. Studies to determine the national audience penetration are conducted weekly or bimonthly. As a rule, they cover all the major productions a firm has in the stage of promotion. Five to ten pictures may be covered in a survey. The results of a long-range national study are presented on Chart 3, which shows the publicity development of M-G-M's "Random Harvest."

Short-range local studies are, as a rule, conducted for a few weeks only. Their purpose is to determine the effect of publicity or advertising for a picture in one town. These studies are conducted before, during, and after the opening of a picture. They

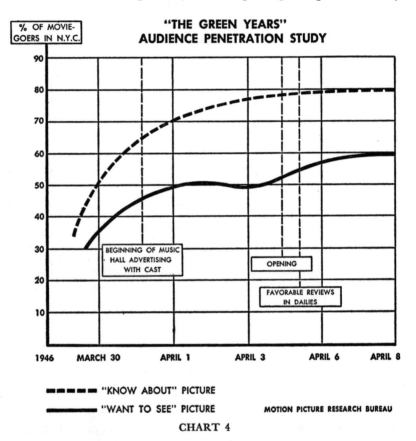

"THE GREEN YEARS"
AUDIENCE PENETRATION STUDY

% OF MOVIE-GOERS IN N.Y.C.

BEGINNING OF MUSIC HALL ADVERTISING WITH CAST

OPENING

FAVORABLE REVIEWS IN DAILIES

1946   MARCH 30   APRIL 1   APRIL 3   APRIL 6   APRIL 8

━ ━ ━ ━ "KNOW ABOUT" PICTURE

━━━━━ "WANT TO SEE" PICTURE   MOTION PICTURE RESEARCH BUREAU

CHART 4

are synchronized with press, radio, and other promotional campaigns. The field interviewing and tabulation for these studies has to be carefully pin-pointed for certain days; they may be conducted weekly, every third day, or every other day of the survey period. An example of a short-range local study may be seen in Chart 4 which reflects the findings of five consecutive surveys carried out just before and after the opening of

M-G-M's "The Green Years" at the Radio City Music Hall in New York City.[4]

Because the Motion Picture Research Bureau and Audience Research, Inc., worked independently, similar terms were used in some cases for different concept. This divergence will be pointed out whenever it occurs in the terminology of the following discussion.

THE ADJUSTED PUBLICITY INDEX

The publicity index used by the Motion Picture Research Bureau is the "adjusted publicity index" which is based on the "raw publicity index."

The raw publicity index is obtained in the following manner: The respondents of a balanced and controlled cross-section of moviegoers are shown a card on which the title or titles of the picture under analysis is printed. The card does not contain any information besides the title. The respondent is given some time to study the card and then is asked by the interviewer whether or not he has heard or read about the picture in question. The proportion of respondents giving an affirmative answer expressed in a percentage figure comprises the raw publicity index.

It must be taken into consideration that some respondents may have said—knowingly or not—that they knew about the picture even though they did not.

To reduce the effect of this factor, the respondents may be asked to give some more concrete information, such as the name of one player in the cast, the type of picture, or the name of the director. In a short-range local study they may be asked if they know where and when the picture is going to be shown. Interviewees who are in a position to identify a picture correctly by mentioning any detail about it beyond the fact that they have heard or read about the title make up a proportion of the

---

[4] According to Audience Research, Inc., 38 per cent of New York City's moviegoers know of the existence of an average "A" feature at the time of its opening in that city. This figure pertains to the end of 1949. The identical ratio in 1946 was 44 per cent (*Film Daily*, January 11, 1950).

sample which is expressed in another index: the "identification" or "correct identification index."

The identification index of the Motion Picture Research Bureau and Audience Research, Inc., term "penetration," or "audience penetration," are two expressions for the same thing. A definition of the Audience Research, Inc., explains penetration as a term used to describe the proportion of United States moviegoers who can prove that they know something about any given motion picture. There are two kinds of penetration reported by Audience Research, Inc., (a) "shown area penetration," and (b) "not shown area penetration."

"Shown area penetration" can be defined as the proportion of moviegoers in areas where the picture has opened who know about it and can identify it in some way. "Not shown area penetration" is the proportion of moviegoers in area where a picture has not played who know something about it.

Studies conducted by the Motion Picture Research Bureau have shown that a true publicity index must lie somewhere between the percentages of persons who claim they have heard about the picture (raw publicity index), and the percentage of persons who have heard about the picture, and who, in addition, can substantiate this fact by giving some concrete information about it (identification index, or the Audience Research, Inc., term penetration).

Obviously, there are some respondents who are reached by publicity and who cannot remember anything but the title. Moreover, many publicity or advertising messages do not contain any information except the title. The fact may be due to the advertising policy laid down for some pictures. In some cases no mention of the cast is made. A typical example of this policy can be seen in the advertising campaign for "The Green Years." Besides Charles Coburn, the picture featured some newcomers who, prior to the release of the movie, could not have had any following to speak of among the moviegoing public. An important phase of the advertising campaign consisted of a series of advertisements in newspapers and other media which contained only the brief statement:

"THE GREEN YEARS"
IS A WONDERFUL MOTION PICTURE

Persons who saw these advertisements but did not learn about this picture from any other source obviously could not indicate either the names of the players or the story type. A "correct identification index" or "index of penetration" would, therefore, not necessarily reflect a true picture of the promotional effort and effect. A similar situation can be seen in connection with certain war pictures. Some were finished and released immediately after the end of the war when the demand for them was very low. Campaigns for some of them, therefore, carefully avoided any reference to the fact that they dealt with war stories, and many respondents could not possibly be familiar with the themes of the productions.

CONFUSION CONTROL

A more reliable indication of the degree to which moviegoers are successfully exposed to advertising and publicity can be seen in the conversion of the raw publicity index to the adjusted publicity index. One method applied is related to techniques of magazine identification studies.

The first objective is to isolate the moviegoers who claim they know about a motion picture even though they do not. It can be anticipated that a percentage of untrue answers may be given partly by mistake and partly on purpose and it is a fair assumption that the proportion of untrue answers remain approximately the same for all penetration surveys.

To determine this proportion of untrue answers it is necessary to conduct special control studies which include titles of nonexistent motion pictures. Special care must be taken that these fictitious titles or test titles do not resemble those of any other pictures, books, or plays released in the United States. The proportion of persons who say they have read or heard of the fictitious titles is generally very low. In one control survey it amounted to 1.2 per cent, in another to 1.7 per cent.[5]

[5] Magazine research figures usually use a confusion control of 4 per cent.

The comparatively low proportion of incorrect statements is also indicated by the fact that actual pictures which were covered by surveys prior to the organized advertising and publicity campaigns are rarely identified by many more than 2 per cent of the interviewees.

From such control surveys the Motion Picture Research Bureau has adopted a "basic reliability deduction" of 2 per cent. Confusion control is applied by deducting 2 per cent of the number of respondents who say that they have heard about a certain picture. The elimination of respondents who are estimated to give incorrect answers must also be accompanied by a subtraction of the basic reliability deduction from the base figure (total number of respondents).

The application of the basic reliability deduction and confusion control procedure may be seen in Table 24.

TABLE 24

Use of Basic Reliability Deduction

			Basic reliability deduction of 2 per cent of 2000 = 40
Number of persons asked	1000	2000	1960
Type of title	ficti-		
	tious	actual	actual
Persons who say they know about the picture	20	400	360
Persons who say they do not know about the picture	980	1600	1600
Publicity index			
(a) Raw	2	20	
(b) Adjusted			18.4

The adjusted publicity index of 18.4 indicates that at the time the survey was conducted, 18.4 per cent of the moviegoers represented by the sample were successfully reached by advertising and publicity.

Despite these adjustments an undue increase of the publicity index may be caused by a similar title of another motion picture or the existence of a play, book, or previous production of the same title.

An example of the first possibility may be seen in the picture

"Ziegfeld Follies of 1946." The original title was "Ziegfeld Follies." Surveys indicated a confusion with a previous production, "The Great Ziegfeld" and other pictures and stage productions on this well known theme. So the title was changed to "Ziegfeld Follies of 1946." The elimination of confusion was indicated by a drop in the publicity index.

Persons familiar with a popular book or play may assume that it will be made into a motion picture. When this influence becomes evident it has to be neutralized by special questions. However, for all practical purposes this appearance is not harmful from the standpoint of the promotion manager. Book and play titles are usually retained because of their publicity value.

THE POTENTIAL AUDIENCE INDEX

The "want-to-see" or potential audience index of the Motion Picture Research Bureau measures the proportion of moviegoers who at the time of the survey not only indicate that they know about a picture but who, in addition, express their intention to see it. The identical statistical method which is used in determining the adjusted publicity index is used for the adjustment of the potential audience index. Chart 4, which shows the publicity development for the "The Green Years," also indicates the increase in the proportion of New York moviegoers who wanted to see this picture.

There is a practical relationship between the publicity and potential audience indexes. Whenever the proportion of moviegoers who express the desire to see a certain picture is too far below the proportion who actually know about it, special investigations are in order which may uncover motives for audience resistance. Respondents who indicate that they do not want to see the picture are asked why they feel this way.

ADVERTISING MEDIA

In addition to the publicity, potential audience, and identification indexes, the Motion Picture Research Bureau usually tries to determine the advertising, publicity, and other promotional media to which the respondents were exposed.

Long-range publicity surveys reflect the employment of different media at different periods of the campaign. The motion picture fans are usually the first ones to register. They draw their information from motion picture magazines and motion picture columns. As time goes by, their relative importance decreases and the average moviegoer gains ground as he learns about the picture from advertisements in national magazines, and on billboards and posters. Finally, when the time of the opening of the picture arrives, newspaper advertising becomes of great importance and usually leads the list.

A typical enumeration of advertising and publicity media to which respondents were exposed is shown below. It is based on a survey taken in New York City just after the opening of a

TABLE 25

MEDIA EXPOSURE

Advertising Media

Newspaper advertising	86%
Preview trailer	15
Radio	22
Posters	32
Subway car cards	49
Railway express trucks	26
National magazines	25
Movie magazines	30

major production in a large first-run theater. The percentages are based on 721 interviews with respondents who came to the theater with the intention of seeing the picture in question, and who were not planning to see "just any movie" on that day.

In addition to the aforementioned types of publicity studies typical of the film industry, a research department of a motion picture firm or an audience research agency usually carries on the type of studies that other advertisers have found of value. To mention a few, there are copy tests, pretesting of individual advertisements, and studies to measure the comparative drawing power of a number of advertisements under consideration. Inasmuch as these latter studies are not typical of film research, they are not discussed here.

TRAILER TESTS

Preview or week-in-advance trailers are one of the most effective promotional media used to stimulate active interest in a motion picture. The main reason for their effectiveness may be seen in the fact that they are trained upon a selected potential audience at the right time and at the right place. Preview trailers in first-run houses are witnessed mainly by first-run house audiences. Preview trailers in a neighborhood theater are seen by patrons of neighborhood theaters.[6] Table 25 does not give a clear enough indication of preview trailers. When we consider that they constitute a very small fraction of the advertising expenditures for a motion picture, the 15 per cent figure becomes more significant.

The purpose of the trailer tests is to ascertain the proportion of the audience who want to see the picture after seeing the preview trailer.

The trailer under observation is run in a theater where the picture it advertises is likely to be shown. Persons who were exposed to it are asked to state whether or not they want to see the picture advertised. Both the persons who want to see the picture and those who do not are asked for their reasons. The focused or depth interview lends itself readily to this type of investigation. If the audience reaction is not satisfactory the trailer may be changed or replaced.

Another method of determining the impact of a trailer consists of a memory test. Persons attending a feature before which a coming attractions trailer has been shown are asked, upon leaving the theater, which picture will follow the current film in this house. A series of such tests revealed that 44 per cent of the respondents can remember the exact title of the coming picture. About 27 per cent recall an approximation of the title, while 29 per cent cannot recollect the coming attraction at all. The last group contains a small number of moviegoers who

---

[6] Television offers a new way of exploiting trailers. This method of advertising is still in the experimental stage and is pioneered by Paramount. It seems to entail considerable promotional values.

were not exposed to the trailer, arriving just after it was shown and leaving before it came on again. Inasmuch as this occurance will hold true for most trailers wherever they are shown, this group of people need not be eliminated from the calculations.

The effectiveness of a trailer may also be expressed by an index which is determined in the same way as the audience appeal index. Persons who see the trailer may be asked to express their degree of interest in the advertised picture with the help of a checklist. Different degrees of interest correspond to different weights which may be used to compute the index.

The effectiveness of trailers, as in the case of most advertising media in the motion picture field, depends not only on the skill with which it is composed but also on the stars, story type, and title of the picture it advertises. Trailers which portray very popular stars will naturally have a greater impact on the audience than trailers which show only a mediocre cast.

THE OPINION LEADER

A chapter about advertising and publicity research would not be complete without devoting a few words to the members in the community who are actively setting opinions about motion pictures by originating and disseminating word-of-mouth publicity. The importance of word-of-mouth publicity may be seen in Table 24 taken from a nationwide study of the Motion Picture Research Bureau. The percentages are based on 1,500 interviews with persons who intended to see a particular picture the last time they went to the movies. Because of multiple mentions, percentages total more than 100.

The importance of word-of-mouth advertising indicated here was confirmed by a study of Columbia University's Bureau of Applied Social Research.[7] This study also attempted to designate the individuals in the community who were most influential in inducing others to attend particular pictures, the opinion leaders.

[7] For a preliminary report on the findings see Lazarsfeld, Paul F., "Audience Research in the Movie Field," *Annals of the American Academy of Political and Social Science*, November, 1947.

It was discovered, for instance, that the advisers on movie matters were apt to be younger than the people they advised. Of the women sampled under thirty-five years old, for instance, 72 per cent claimed that they gave advice to women over thirty-five. When the women over thirty-five were asked who had advised them about movies, 55 per cent acknowledged advice from women younger than thirty-five years of age.[8] It was also dis-

TABLE 26

	Sources from which respondent learned about last picture	The most influential source
Hearsay	39%	17%
Advertising in newspapers and magazines	44	12
Reviews	36	17
Trailer	27	8
Advertising in/on theater	20	3
Radio	12	2
Outdoor advertising	3	1
Other	5	...
None	...	40
Total	100%	100%

covered that influences, in regard to movies, tended to flow socially on a horizontal plane rather than from the top layers down.

Movie leaders show up a large number of characteristics, some quite obvious and some less so. The opinion leaders, of course, are those who go to the movies frequently. They are also those who are otherwise especially concerned with movies. For instance, they read many more movie magazines than other groups in the population. But although they are movie fans, they have other interests also. Altogether, they do more radio listening and read more magazines [9] and their communications habits are more active than is true of people in the same age, income, and education group who are not movie leaders. Furthermore, movie opinion leadership seems to be related to a special inclination toward social activity. Leaders telephone

[8] *Seventeen* magazine in its survey "Teenage Girls and Their Motion Picture Habits" (New York: 1948) finds that families almost always follow their daughters choices in the selection of motion pictures.

[9] See Chapter 10.

and visit a great deal and show other signs of active social participation.

While opinion leaders give advice to other people, they are themselves unusually impressed by the movies. It was found that they are more likely to attribute special effects on their own lives to the movies. Finally, it is of some practical interest to know that these influencers of others are more likely than others to be influenced by the promotional activities of the movie industry. They report more often that they went to a movie because they heard it discussed over the radio, and are likely to look for specific information on pictures in newspapers and magazines.

Part Three: Studies of general problems

CHAPTER *7* *The motion picture audience*

The most primitive kind of communications research pertains to the extent and nature of the audience. In respect to movie research, few thorough attempts have been made to obtain reliable information on this subject. Eric Johnston, president of the Motion Picture Association of America, came forward with a statement to this effect, when he submitted his first annual report to the association.[1]

The Motion Picture industry probably knows less about itself than any other major industry in the United States. The industry had grown so fast that it hardly has had a time to measure its own growth. Consequently it possesses today only a smattering of information about its own operations. Much of the statistical data published about this industry is based on hearsay, personal opinion, the casual impressions of persons unfamiliar with the business or the natural exuberance of born promoters. . . .

The purpose of this chapter is to discuss what little has been done in the analysis of the film audience as such. It must be borne in mind that this audience is subject to continuous changes of both a seasonal and a structural character. These

[1] Johnston, Eric, *The Motion Picture on the Threshold of a Decisive Decade* (New York: 1946).

changes were even more acute in the periods before and during the war and are continuing to be of great impact in the postwar period. The few figures available which were obtained from surveys conducted between 1941 and 1946 should be regarded with reservation.

THE VOLUME OF THE MOTION PICTURE AUDIENCE

The size of the motion picture audience may be interpreted in different ways. To avoid confusion, a clarification of the terminology may be of value. The terms most in use are:

(a) The potential audience
(b) The actual audience
(c) The average weekly motion picture attendance
(d) The maximum number of admissions or potential audience for a motion picture
(e) The average number of admissions of a motion picture

The potential audience includes all persons living in this country who are physically and economically able to attend motion pictures. Various industry estimates put the potential audience in the neighborhood of 105 million persons out of the national population of 150 million. The balance of 45 million are either too old, too young, living at places too distant from a theater, confined to institutions, hospitals, economically unable to attend, sick, or otherwise incapacitated. Audience Research, Inc., found at the beginning of 1946 that 81 million people over twelve years of age have attended motion pictures at least once in their lifetime. This figure bears out the industry estimates which include children under twelve years of age.

The actual audience, many times referred to simply as "the audience," covers the section of the potential audience which is composed of actual moviegoers. There is, however, no agreement as to what constitutes a "moviegoer."

The Motion Picture Research Bureau considers as moviegoers respondents who average at least one motion picture attendance a month. A study revealed that only seven out of ten potential patrons attend at this rate. It was estimated, therefore, that there are about seventy million people in this country, of all ages, who comprise the actual audience. Audience Research, Inc., found that there are fifty-six million Americans over twelve years of age who can be considered moviegoers, according to this organization's definition of a moviegoer as a person who attends at least once every three weeks. Both calculations were computed at the beginning of 1946.

In a study done in "Central City" by Columbia University's Bureau of Applied Social Research[2] the following ratio of attendance for women was recorded, representing answers to the question "How often do you go to the movies?"

	Number	Per cent
One or more times a week	268	37
One to three times a month	193	27
Few times a year, hardly ever	176	25
Never	73	11
Total	710	100

From these figures we could label as moviegoers 89 per cent (excluding only those who never go), 64 per cent (counting all who go at least once a month), or 37 per cent (considering those who attend at least once a week).

The difference between the actual and potential audience is made up of people who could be moviegoers but who do not care to see motion pictures and who attend only rarely. There are about thirty million occasional or non-moviegoers in this country. To the author's knowledge no large-scale studies were ever made to determine exactly why so many persons do not attend or attend only very seldom. However, at the time this was written the Motion Picture Association of America had a project under consideration which would provide for detailed studies of both moviegoers and non-moviegoers.

The average weekly motion picture attendance refers to the number of tickets sold, but not the number of individuals who attend, because any one person may attend more than once.

The available figures for the average weekly motion picture

[2] See Lazarsfeld, P. F., "Audience Research in the Movie Field" *Annals of the American Academy of Political and Social Science,* November, 1947.

attendance show wide variance. Standard and Poor reports place the average weekly attendance above the 100-million mark for 1945.[3] According to the *Film Daily Year Book* in 1946, which derives its information from U. S. Treasury tax figures, the average is 95 million for the same year. Audience Research, Inc., reported that the average weekly full-price admission in the nation's theaters was 66 million at the beginning of 1946. This would be an increase of over 22 per cent since 1940, when Gallup estimated the full-price admission total as 54 million and the *Film Daily Year Book* reported 80 million. (The *Film Daily Year Book's* estimate for average weekly attendances in 1948 is 90 million.)

The maximum number of admissions for any motion picture ever released was obtained by David O. Selznick's "Gone with the Wind." The picture sold more than sixty-one million tickets in the course of its four releases. The number of individuals who saw the picture is placed in the vicinity of fifty-one million, many patrons seeing it two or more times.

The number of admissions obtained for "Gone with the Wind" is often considered as the maximum potential audience for an individual motion picture.

The *average number of admissions* for an average "A" picture is put at thirteen million by Audience Research, Inc., for 1948,[4] as compared to fifteen million in 1947 and sixteen million in 1946. Calculating an average admission of forty-five cents, this would mean that the average "A" picture's grosses amount to about $5,850,000. Audience Research, Inc., also figures that there are 5,400,000 persons in this country who see practically every picture.

Social and economic trends show that the motion picture audience in the United States will probably experience a steady growth. A study conducted by the 20th Century Fund [5] indi-

[3] Negro theater patronage in the United States accounts for approximately five and one-half million of the weekly film attendance. Between 1937 and 1949 the number of houses catering to Negroes increased from about 400 to more than 900. Besides the regular 35 mm. theaters there are a large number of 16 mm. enterprises operating especially for Negroes (*Film Daily*, August 15, 1949).

[4] *Variety*, February 23, 1949.

[5] *Film Daily*, January 29, 1948.

cated an enlargement of the domestic market for films because
of growth of population, continued reduction in the work week,
wider distribution of national income, and changes in the
spending pattern of the average family, with a greater proportion of expenditures going into recreation. Chart 5 gives a
graphic account of these developments. Motion pictures are cited

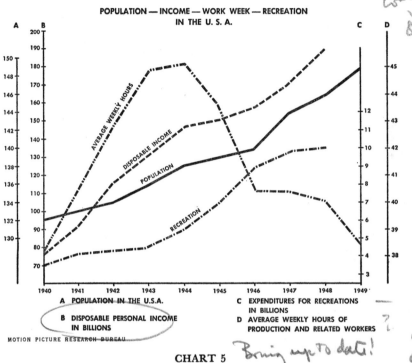

POPULATION — INCOME — WORK WEEK — RECREATION IN THE U. S. A.

A POPULATION IN THE U.S.A.

B DISPOSABLE PERSONAL INCOME IN BILLIONS

C EXPENDITURES FOR RECREATIONS IN BILLIONS

D AVERAGE WEEKLY HOURS OF PRODUCTION AND RELATED WORKERS

MOTION PICTURE RESEARCH BUREAU

CHART 5

in this study as among the "insensitive industries"—those whose
revenues show a change of less than 8 per cent when there
is a 10 per cent decline in total consumer income. Admissions
are said to be relatively more stable in the face of adverse economic conditions than, for instance, sales of autos, clothing,
radios, phonographs, electrical appliances, and household equipment. During 1930–33 and again in 1937–38, films' share of
total consumer expenditures increased, while those of some so-

called necessities were losing ground. Projecting the results of current trends into the 1950–60 decade, the survey cites a number of factors to indicate the growth potential of motion pictures. National income in 1950, assuming that the economy continues to operate at a high level, will be 36 per cent higher than in 1940, and by 1960 will be up another 15 per cent, excluding the effect of price increases since 1940. Even more significant to the film industry is the anticipated wider distribution of national income.

Total consumer spending in 1950 is expected to be 24.6 per cent above the 1940 level, in terms of 1940 dollars, and by 1960 is expected to be 44 per cent above 1940. Consumer spending for recreation, it is estimated, will increase at an even faster pace—rising 32 per cent by 1950 in comparison with 1940, and increasing 58.8 per cent by 1960. Films, as the largest single economic factor in recreation and entertainment, can be expected to absorb nearly a fifth of all money spent on recreation. An increased future attendance may also be seen in another development which, however, would need further investigation. Many of today's older persons could not acquire the movie habit while they were young because they had no chance to see pictures then. This holds especially true for the foreign-born population. It may be safely assumed that a larger proportion of older people will attend motion pictures in the years to come because of conditioning to this form of entertainment in their youth. Beyond this, there are still other factors which may result in higher future attendance frequencies such as the increasing proportion of urban population, the shorter work week leaving more time for recreation, and a comparatively new appearance in the motion picture market, the 16 mm. film which will try to bring pictures to small isolated communities which could not maintain regular theaters. Also drive-in theaters are creating additional audiences. Television is beginning to make itself felt in the field of entertainment. This medium, however, is too new to permit a prediction of how it will affect the motion picture attendance of tomorrow.

AUDIENCE COMPOSITION

Various independent studies have been conducted by different agencies, yielding some information about the composition of the motion picture audience. The results of most studies agree on the following facts about audience composition:

Male and female patrons attend at about equal rates.
Younger people attend more frequently than older people.
Persons in higher socio-economic brackets attend more frequently than those in lower levels.
The more years a person has spent in school, the more frequently he sees motion pictures.

In the following pages statistics are quoted from a number of research studies which will try to substantiate these claims. An exact knowledge of the audience composition is of special interest to the researcher in the motion picture field since he needs this information in the construction of his sample.[6]

Sex

Many persons connected with the motion picture industry have been under the impression that the majority of the audience is composed of women. Some have estimated 65 per cent of the moviegoers as female, others as high as 70 per cent. These opinions may have originated from observations made in some theaters or localities where such a ratio might actually have existed. It is even possible, though not probable, that this proportion held true at some time in the past.

The erroneous assumption that the majority of the film audience is composed of women resulted in the fact that some motion picture companies catered to the tastes of female patrons both in their productions and in the promotional campaigns, a policy which may have resulted in a considerable loss of business among male customers. But all research studies conducted within the last five years or so point clearly to the fact that the average monthly movie attendance of men and women is practi-

[6] See Appendix.

cally equal. While slightly fewer women than men are non-moviegoers, various studies found men better represented in the very high attendance frequency brackets (attending ten times a month and more).

In a survey conducted in the metropolitan area of New York in December, 1941, based on 508 interviews, the following average monthly motion picture attendance was found: For men, 3.70 and for women, 3.75.[7]

Women have only a slightly higher average attendance rate. We see, however, a greater proportion of men in the very high frequency of attendance category in Table 27.

TABLE 27
FREQUENCY OF MONTHLY ATTENDANCE OF MEN AND WOMEN

Times per month	Men	Women	Total
0	24.7%	20.6%	22.6%
1 to 2	21.2	17.4	19.3
3 to 5	26.3	35.1	30.7
6 to 9	16.0	19.4	17.7
10 and over	11.8	7.5	9.7
Total	100.0%	100.0%	100.0%

Women thus led in the three-to-five and the six-to-nine per month categories but men were more likely to attend more than ten times per month.

A statewide study conducted by F. L. Whan of the University of Wichita and H. B. Summers of Kansas State College [8] is a further corroboration that male and female attendance is about equal. The survey covered the state of Iowa, where more than nine thousand interviews were conducted in the spring of 1942.

Each person interviewed in the Iowa study was asked how many times he had attended a moving picture theater during the thirty days preceding the interview. Whan reported that no significant differences were found between the attendance of people living in cities, in villages, and on farms. All attended with the same degree of frequency. The following table gives

[7] Handel, Leo, *Studies of the Motion Picture Audience.*
[8] Whan, F. L., and Summers, H. B., *The 1942 Iowa Radio Audience Survey* (Des Moines: 1942).

the percentages of all men and women interviewed in this study falling into each classification. The figures show little variance in the attendance figures for men and women.

According to the findings of Audience Research, Inc., also, men and women moviegoers are about equal in numbers. During the war women were for some time actually in the majority. As soon as the men came back from overseas the equal balance was re-established.

FREQUENCY OF MONTHLY ATTENDANCE BY MEN AND
WOMEN: IOWA SURVEY

	Men	Women
Did not attend	49.7%	49.2%
Attended once	15.5	16.8
Two to three times	16.6	17.2
Four to five times	11.1	11.4
More than five times	7.1	5.4
Total	100.0%	100.0%

Beside these serious efforts to establish facts by means of scientific samplings we find, every now and then, reports from unrepresentative audience groups which claim different results. Outstanding examples are the reports of the Women's Institute of Audience Reactions.[9] The Institute questioned about five thousand women from coast to coast, and concluded that 65 per cent of the film audience consists of women. In another report the Institute published findings which purported to show that practically all men who go to the motion pictures were in some way or another influenced to do so by women.

Even though, for all practical purposes, men and women attend at an equal rate, studies have revealed that women are usually better versed than men on movie topics. The following table refers to five different surveys conducted by the Motion Picture Research Bureau at different times. It shows the number of pictures covered by each survey and the extent to which women were better informed about the different pictures than men, with regard to cast, story, opening theater, etc. Each study is based on interviews with about two thousand persons.

Another indication that women are better versed than men in

9 *Film Daily*, November 17, 1942.

news about motion pictures was corroborated by a readership analysis of *Time* magazine.[10] A study among equal numbers of men and women subscribers revealed the intensity of readership, department by department, by sexes.

TABLE 28

INFORMATION ABOUT MOTION PICTURES

	Surveys				
	1	*2*	*3*	*4*	*5*
Number of pictures covered by survey	10	9	9	8	9
Number of pictures women knew more about than men	9	7	5	5	5
Number of pictures men knew more about than women	1	1	4	2	1
Number of pictures about which men and women were equally well informed	...	1	...	1	3

The readership figures for each department were based on 2,400 personal interviews. A breakdown of the figures pertaining to the "Cinema" department showed that this section is read by 121 women readers for every hundred male readers.

Age

A knowledge of the age stratifications of the motion picture audience should be of value to producers, advertisers, and exhibitors. Research work conducted to determine the effects of age on attendance is also spotty in character. Continuous studies would be of great value in this field.

All surveys point to the fact that young people attend more frequently than older people. Many of the older persons, as pointed out before, did not have the opportunity to become motion picture fans when they were young, simply because the film industry itself is young. It is probable that the higher age groups of tomorrow will not show the same drastic difference in attendance frequency. Lazarsfeld lists several additional factors.

Movie-going is essentially a social activity, and young people are more likely to band together for the purpose of entertainment.

[10] *Time,* December 8, 1947, p. 106.

Then, for movies one has to leave the house, which probably becomes more distasteful as one grows older. Finally, radio programs and reading material offer a greater variety of choices, and each age group can select from these media items that interest them. The supply of movies, however, is much smaller and the variety more limited, and they are patterned to the tastes of younger people.[11]

The New York study of the Motion Picture Research Bureau obtained the following figures for age breakdowns.

TABLE 29

FREQUENCY OF ATTENDANCE BY AGE GROUPS

(a) Total

Age Group	Times per month
10 to 24 years	4.6
25 to 34 years	4.0
35 to 49 years	2.9
50 and over	2.0
Total	3.7

(b) Proportion of persons who attended over four times a month

Age Group	
10 to 24 years	43%
25 to 34 years	35
35 to 49 years	23
50 and over	15
Total	33%

The Iowa survey indicates the rate of attendance by age groups in Table 30.

TABLE 30

FREQUENCY OF ATTENDANCE BY AGE GROUPS: IOWA SURVEY

Age groups	Times per month					
	0	1	2–3	4–5	Over 5	Total
Men:						
15 to 20 years	9.2%	10.7%	21.8%	27.2%	31.0%	100.0%
21 to 35 years	32.4	17.9	20.8	17.6	11.4	100.0
36 to 50 years	54.4	15.6	18.2	8.3	3.4	100.0
Over 50 years	73.4	12.7	8.3	3.7	1.9	100.0
Women:						
15 to 20 years	15.6	8.2	23.8	27.5	24.9	100.0
21 to 35 years	35.8	19.1	22.3	15.1	7.6	100.0
36 to 50 years	51.5	18.8	16.5	9.6	3.5	100.0
Over 50 years	72.8	11.4	9.3	5.8	0.7	100.0

[11] Lazarsfeld, P. F., "Audience Research in the Movie Field," *loc. cit.*

A survey conducted by Link and Hopf [12] which was based on a sample of four thousand persons had, among other objectives, the purpose of determining the number of respondents who had seen a motion picture on the day before the interview. The age breakdown showed the following pattern:

	15–19	*20–29*	*30–39*	*40–49*	*50–59*	*60 plus*	Total
Went to movies yesterday	27%	16%	11%	8%	9%	6%	12%

According to an estimate by Dr. J. S. List, a consulting psychologist, a fifth of the nation's theatergoers cease to be regular patrons when they reach the age of forty.[13] List contends further that 75 per cent of the patrons are lost to the industry when they reach sixty, and 98 per cent when they reach seventy. He sees the cause for this diminishing market in the lack of understanding of adult tastes on the part of the producers, and the failure of the exhibitors to cultivate this section of the public.

Socio-Economic Levels

According to a report [14] of the United States Department of Labor, most people spend more money for motion pictures than for any other recreational activity. The only exception are families in the highest income bracket ($10,000 and over) who spend more for games and sports equipment than for films. Table 31 shows the outlays for motion picture admissions by urban families and single consumers for 1941. It can be seen that the expenditures for motion pictures increase with the annual incomes. It has to be borne in mind, however, that the rate of attendance does not increase in proportion to the expenditures for admissions, since people in the higher income group brackets usually pay more per ticket than people at the lesser income levels.

[12] Link, Henry C., and Hopf, Harry Arthur, *People and Books* (New York: Book Industry Committee, 1946).

[13] *Film Daily*, July 16, 1941.

[14] United States Department of Labor, *Family Spending and Saving in Wartime*, Bulletin No. 822. The survey was conducted with the purpose of recording the income, expenditures, and savings of a cross-section of the nation's families and single consumers. 3,100 cases were surveyed in 62 cities across the country. The study covered twelve months of the year 1941 and three months of 1942.

TABLE 31

AVERAGE AMOUNT SPENT FOR RECREATIONS BY URBAN FAMILIES AND SINGLE CONSUMERS IN 1941 (TWELVE MONTHS)

ANNUAL MONEY INCOME CLASSES

Annual income	-$500	$500-1000	$1000-1500	$1500-2000	$2000-2500	$2500-3000	$3000-5000	$5000-10,000	$10,000+
Average expenditure for recreation, total	$20.68	$19.37	$34.53	$54.02	$78.23	$104.46	$154.84	$296.58	$603.32
Paid admission to movies	$3.31	$7.15	$14.00	$20.68	$24.88	$36.71	$49.52	$57.02	$71.23
Other paid admissions[1]	.33	1.34	2.23	3.36	5.60	5.05	11.79	25.80	66.84
Games and sports equipment[2]	3.54	1.67	3.04	5.26	9.73	12.53	25.39	42.56	131.43
Radio and radio phonograph purchase[3]	1.61	2.48	3.06	5.71	6.36	10.80	11.78	13.99	20.76
Radio, tubes, batteries, repairs	.22	.25	.55	.57	.77	1.12	1.51	2.55	4.59
Phonographs	0	0	.08	.05	.11	.39	.43	.29	0
Musical instruments	0	0	.84	.63	5.66	6.49	3.10	29.38	10.76
Sheet music, phonograph records	.15	.14	.29	.48	.59	1.59	2.74	6.32	13.42
Cameras, films, photo supplies	.28	.28	.54	1.26	2.54	2.40	6.00	18.49	39.50
Children's toys, play equipment	.11	.41	1.47	3.22	3.07	3.73	2.59	12.05	15.00
Pets (purchase and care)[4]	0	.63	1.91	1.64	3.16	4.15	6.86	12.36	21.29
Entertaining in and out of homes[5]	.43	.85	3.55	6.83	7.65	11.14	21.51	39.89	99.10
Dues to social and recreational clubs[6]	.47	.88	1.52	2.70	4.37	4.89	8.18	31.45	86.89
Other[7]	10.23	3.29	1.45	1.63	3.74	3.47	3.44	4.43	22.51

[1] Includes fees for attendance at lectures, plays, concerts, baseball games, etc.
[2] Includes athletic fees paid at school, hunting licenses, rental fees, purchase price, and expenses connected with the upkeep and maintenance of boats and horses used primarily for recreation.
[3] Gross price minus trade-in allowance.
[4] Includes medical care and license fees.
[5] Includes expense for bridge prizes, favors, and decorations other than flowers.
[6] Includes membership in YMCA, lodges, and golf clubs.
[7] Includes net gambling losses, expense for Christmas trees, and for hobbies, etc.

Other figures pertaining to the effect of income in motion picture attendance were obtained in the course of the previously quoted New York study of the Motion Picture Research Bureau.

TABLE 32
FREQUENCY OF ATTENDANCE BY INCOME

(a) Total

Income group	Times per month
High	3.7
Middle	4.0
Low	3.3

(b) Proportion of persons who attended over four times a month

Income group	
High	30.2%
Middle	36.8
Low	27.1

The figures in Table 32 give the medium income group a slight lead over the high income group, bearing out the assumption that higher expenditures need not mean more frequent attendance.

Education

Two research surveys yielded valuable information about the effect of education on motion picture attendance. Both indicate that persons who went to grade school only are less frequent moviegoers than those who went to high school and college.

The previously mentioned canvass by Link and Hopf permitted a breakdown of the respondents by educational levels. It shows that persons with high school education attend more often than persons who went to grade school only. The figures show also a tapering off of attendance by college people.

	Grade school	High school	College	Total
Went to movies yesterday	10%	15%	11%	12%

The Iowa survey, Table 33, also indicates that persons with only grade school education go to the motion pictures least frequently. However, in this study the figures indicate that persons with college education attend more often than people with either grade school or high school background.

In general the findings seem to indicate a misconception on the part of some producers who feel that they have to "play down" to the lowest intellectual level to make a motion picture a financial success.

TABLE 33

FREQUENCY OF ATTENDANCE BY EDUCATION: IOWA SURVEY

| | | | Times per month | | | |
	0	1	2–3	4–5	Over 5	Total
Men						
Attended college	35.3%	16.3%	21.1%	17.0%	10.3%	100.0%
Attended high school	39.9	17.0	20.5	13.0	9.5	100.0
Grade school only	65.4	13.1	11.4	6.8	3.3	100.0
Women						
Attended college	36.0	19.1	23.8	13.7	7.5	100.0
Attended high school	42.5	18.2	19.4	13.4	6.4	100.0
Grade school only	66.7	13.5	10.2	7.0	2.5	100.0

THE INTERRELATION OF FACTORS

Since age, income, and education are variables interrelated among themselves, it is probable that no one of them operates singly to produce differences in movie attendance. People of higher income, for instance, are apt also to be better educated, so that the increased attendance that we find among more highly educated groups may actually be a function of the economic status of these groups, or, contrarily, the low attendance rate among the poor may be caused by the relative lack of education. Most likely, both factors are operative in combination.

Age and education are also related. The Bureau of Applied Social Research's "Central City" study provides a cross-analysis of these two factors for the sample of women.

Anyone attending the movies at least once a week was defined as a moviegoer.[15]

[15] Paul F. Lazarsfeld "Audience Research in the Movie Field," *loc. cit.*

The age differences are pronounced on all educational levels. Only among the very old people, however, does education appear to play a part, the uneducated going markedly less frequently to the movies. Even here there may be a special reason

TABLE 34

PERCENTAGE WHO GO TO MOVIES AT LEAST ONCE A WEEK

	High school education	Less than high school education
Age groups:		
Under 25	69%	69%
25 to 44	40	42
Over 44	31	11

for the education difference, since the low educated, older group are apt to be composed largely of immigrants who would still have language handicaps.

ATTENDANCE HABITS OF CHILDREN

Most studies of motion picture audiences exclude children. Usually only persons above ten or twelve years are subject to the inquiries. But about 10 per cent of the tickets are bought by children between six and twelve years of age.

To the author's knowledge, little work was done to determine attendance habits of children, aside from a very detailed analysis made by Edgar Dale of motion picture habits of children in 1928 and 1930.[16] The fieldwork was conducted in Ohio. Even though the study is old it is worthwhile to include a brief digest of Dale's findings in this chapter.

The major aim of this study was to determine the frequency of attendance of school children at commercial motion pictures in relation to age, sex, companions, time of day, day of attendance, and program offerings most frequently viewed.

The facts were obtained in two ways. First, observers stationed near the ticket-taker in theaters noted the proportion of the audience which was composed of children under the age of seven, from seven to thirteen, from fourteen to twenty, from twenty-one and over. For approximately three months a group of observers systematically checked the attendance of fifteen

[16] Dale, Edgar, *Children's Attendance of Motion Pictures* (Macmillan, 1935).

Columbus theaters. This number represented the sampling of about one-third of the theaters, and each type of theater was appropriately represented. Each theater was checked for a week. The composition of the Columbus movie audience was as follows:

Age	
Under 7	2.8%
7 to 13	11.8
14 to 20	22.1
21 and over	63.3
Total	100.0%

A second method was the use of an inquiry blank from which the research workers secured attendance data on approximately fifty-five thousand children from the kindergarten through the twelfth grade, in fifty different communities in Ohio and several communities in another state. They discovered that in a seven-day period 16,750 Ohio boys and girls in the primary grades attended 7,008 times, or an average of .42 times a week. The 35,453 boys and girls in grades four to twelve attended 35,155 times or an average (mean) of almost exactly one attendance a week. Twenty-two per cent of the group in the primary grades reported to their teachers that they never attended.

The most popular days for motion picture attendance by children are, in order of popularity, Saturday, Sunday, Friday, Wednesday, Monday, Tuesday, and Thursday. About one-third of all attendances were on Saturday, one-fourth on Sunday, and one-eighth on Friday. Almost three-fourths of the attendances, therefore, are concentrated on the weekend.

If the popularity of a type of film can be judged properly by the frequency with which it is viewed more than once, the relative appeal of the main picture, the newsreel, and the comedy short is indicated in the following table.

	Mean Attendances		
	Boys	*Girls*	*Both*
Feature:			
Main picture	1.22	1.19	1.21
Newsreel	1.22	1.15	1.19
Comedy short	1.31	1.22	1.26

If the child had viewed each feature only once, the mean in each case would be represented by the figure 1.0. Boys spend more time in the movies than girls. Both groups spend more time viewing the comedy short than either of the other two features of the program. The time spent in re-viewing these three features decreases with increasing maturity.

The companions of children at the movies are distributed in percentages as follows:

	Boys	*Girls*	*Both*
Father	2.63%	2.63%	2.63%
Mother	3.65	9.13	6.13
Father and mother	6.37	9.83	7.94
Brother and sister	14.81	18.99	16.70
Own friends	34.77	35.77	35.22
Someone else	11.48	14.77	12.96
No companion	25.18	7.89	17.37
No data	1.11	.99	1.05
Total	100.00%	100.00%	100.00%

Girls are accompanied by their parents almost twice as often as boys. Of the total attendance for both boys and girls, 16.7 per cent are with brother and sister as companions. More children go with their own friends than with any other group. Three times as many boys go alone to the movies as girls.

The time of the day when boys and girls from the age of eight to nineteen attend is as follows:

	Boys	*Girls*	*Both*
Morning	2.90%	2.41%	2.68%
Afternoon	30.02	33.15	31.43
Evening	67.08	64.44	65.89
Total	100.00%	100.00%	100.00%

The morning attendance is indeed slight, less than 3 per cent. About one-third of the attendance is in the afternoon, and two-thirds in the evening. There is a tendency for girls to go more frequently in the afternoon and less frequently in the evening.

One of the few studies giving information on the attitudes of adolescents in matters of entertainment was carried out by the Gilbert Youth Research Organization. The sample covered boys among the age groups of thirteen to eighteen and the interest in motion pictures was only the incidental result of one question in the survey. The question "What are your hobbies, your outside interests?" shows the importance of motion pictures even though "sports" are far in the lead. Table 35 represents the detailed results.[17]

TABLE 35

HOBBIES OF BOYS BETWEEN THIRTEEN AND EIGHTEEN YEARS OF AGE

	First Choice	Second Choice	Third Choice
Sports	70%	10%	4%
Dancing	5	15	14
Movies	6	41	18
Reading	3	10	16
Swing music	5	8	18
Collections	3	3	4
Something else	3	4	4
No answer	5	9	22
Total	100%	100%	100%

British social research made some interesting inroads into the little-explored area of children audiences. J. P. Mayer in his *Sociology of Films* (London) devotes three chapters to the young moviegoers ("Impressions and Reflections on Children's Cinema Clubs," "Children and Adolescents in the Cinemas," "Children in the Cinema"). The findings and conclusions are largely based on personal observations by the author and on the "essay method" which gave the contributors a free field to express themselves. Another approach to determine children's attitudes and preferences was used by Sidney L. Bernstein, chairman of the Granada Theatres, Ltd., in association with Dr. Emanuel Miller, well known British child psychiatrist. Bernstein and Miller attempted to obtain their information by distributing questionnaires among the children attending the Saturday morning matinees.

THE MOTION PICTURE ON FARMS

The motion picture is playing an increasing role in the lives of farmers, according to a study conducted by Elmo Roper late

[17] Gilbert, Eugene, "What the Teen-Age Consumer Thinks," *The Boys' Outfitter*, September, 1946.

in 1946.[18] Even though the particular survey does not represent a cross-section of all farmers in America, the results can be considered significant. The study in question was based on interviews conducted in seven selected counties in Minnesota, South Dakota, Wisconsin, and Iowa.

Few farmers live within easy walking distance of their nearest moving picture theater. Unlike many persons living in large or small towns, they must in most cases travel to see a show. The Roper survey revealed the distances farmers have to cover to reach the nearest theater in the counties where the interviews were recorded.

Miles from home	Farmers
1 to 5	47.6%
5 to 10	36.0
10 to 15	12.7
More than 15	2.5
No answer	1.2
Total	100.0%

Despite these distances, farmers attend motion pictures quite frequently. This is indicated by the following figures, which incidentally come very close to the previously cited Iowa survey —which also covered a predominantly agricultural state.

Frequency of attendance	Farmers
0	50.7%
1 to 3	38.6
4 to 7	8.7
No answer	2.0
Total	100.0%

Roper investigated also the part other media of communications play in farm areas and found that 90 per cent of the people who live in small towns of less than 2,500 population read a daily paper; and 85.6 per cent of those who actually live on farms also reported they read a daily newspaper. More than 90 per cent own a radio and 69 per cent reported the possession of a telephone.

[18] Roper, Elmo, "What People Are Thinking," *New York Herald Tribune,* October 24, 1946.

THE ATTENDANCE UNIT

The "attendance unit" is a term indicating the number and relationship of persons who go to see a motion picture together. The audience for a motion picture as a whole is composed of these attendance units. A discussion of them is, therefore, part of the section audience composition.

A few studies have been conducted to ascertain the nature of the attendance unit. Most of the more reliable ones have the following results in common:

The most frequently encountered attendance unit consists of two persons. A considerable part of the audience is composed of persons who attend alone. Men are more inclined to go and see a picture without a companion than women.

The Motion Picture Research Bureau conducted a research study in February, 1943, which, among other objectives, had the purpose of analyzing the attendance unit. A sample of about 2,200 moviegoers was questioned in thirty-nine towns. The percentages in Tables 36 and 37 are based on the findings of this survey.

TABLE 36

QUESTION: THE LAST TIME YOU WENT TO THE MOVIES, DID YOU GO ALONE OR WITH ANOTHER PERSON?

	Men	Women	Total
Alone	30%	14%	22%
With another person	70	86	78
Total	100%	100%	100%

After the elimination of non-moviegoers, the first key question of the study established the proportion of persons who attended alone and of those who attended with other persons.

The tendency for women to go to movies accompanied by others more frequently than men is clearly indicated here. The next step was to determine the number of co-attendants. This information is contained in Table 37.

As Table 37 clearly indicates, both sexes tend to see movies with only one companion.[19]

TABLE 37
QUESTION: HOW MANY PERSONS ATTENDED WITH YOU?

Number of co-attendants	Men	Women	Total
0	30%	14%	22%
1	58	71	65
2	8	11	9
3	2	2	2
4	1	1	1
more than 4	1	1	1
Total	100%	100%	100%

Respondents who visited the theater in the company of another person were also asked with whom they attended, to determine the composition of the attendance unit (see Table 38).

TABLE 38 [1]
QUESTION: WITH WHOM DID YOU GO?

	Men	Women	Total
Father	4%	3%	4%
Mother	7	9	8
Husband, wife	33	32	33
Son, daughter	7	13	10
Other relative	5	12	9
Sweetheart	10	7	8
Just friend	42	42	42

[1]Due to multiple mentions, percentages add up to more than 100.

At the same time an attempt was made to get an idea as to who was responsible for the last theater visit upon which the entire inquiry was projected. Only those interviewees who had attended with only one other person were asked the question. A tabulation of the answers is shown in Table 39.

The results show that children are the driving power behind the motion picture attendance when they attend with either or both parents. Husbands and wives stated, in the majority of cases covered, that the decision about this visit to the cinema was made mutually. Whenever that was not the case, however,

[19] See different attendance pattern for drive-in theaters in chapter 13.

TABLE 39

QUESTION: WHOSE IDEA WAS IT TO GO TO SEE THE PICTURE YOU SAW, YOURS OR
THE OTHER PERSON'S?

	Respondent	Co-attendant	Mutually	Total
		Men		
Co-attendant:				
Father	40%	40%	20%	100%
Mother	57	31	12	100
Wife	15	34	51	100
Son, daughter	27	53	20	100
Other relative	43	14	43	100
Girl friend	24	33	43	100
Just friend	28	16	56	100
		Women		
Co-attendant:				
Father	45%	5%	50%	100%
Mother	15	22	63	100
Husband	22	22	56	100
Son, daughter	18	49	33	100
Other relative	30	26	44	100
Boy friend	30	11	59	100
Just friend	20	20	60	100

the wife was usually more responsible for the particular motion
picture visit in question than the husband. An almost identical
situation prevails when a man and his girl friend are planning to
see a picture.

WAR INFLUENCE ON MOTION PICTURE ATTENDANCE

It was pointed out at the beginning of this chapter that the
volume and composition of the motion picture audience as a
whole is subject to continuous change. There are three different
kinds of influences which operate to produce these changes.

      (a) Seasonal influences
      (b) Structural influences
      (c) Special influences

This field was never thoroughly explored. We know the
character of seasonal influences through the fact that more
tickets are sold in winter than during the summer when the
competition is keener from other types of recreation, especially

sports. Structural influences, as the one caused by the steady increase of the population in the United States, are more difficult to recognize because they evolve rather slowly. Special influences such as a war are clearly noticeable even though many facts are usually misinterpreted due to their relative complexity.

The Motion Picture Research Bureau conducted one local study to determine the influence of the war on motion picture attendance. The survey was made in New York in August, 1942. About five hundred interviews with moviegoers were recorded.

For the purpose of the analysis the respondents were divided into three groups. The first group consisted of respondents who at the time of the survey attended more frequently than they had in summer 1941. The second group was made up of persons who attended less frequently in 1942 while the third group covered respondents whose attendance frequency had not changed. The study revealed the following changes in attendance frequencies.

CHANGE IN AVERAGE ATTENDANCE FREQUENCIES
SUMMER 1942–SUMMER 1941

Attendance in Summer 1942	
More frequent	22%
Less frequent	19
No change	59
Total	100%

The interviews were continued only with persons who stated that they attended either more or less frequently. They were asked the reasons for the change in attendance. The answers showed that the changes were due both to structural influences and to the special effects of the war. It will be noticed that the same influences may cause either an increase or a decrease of attendance.

War developments resulted in increased attendance because of the following most frequently mentioned reasons:

Many people had better jobs and more money to spend.

Workers on nightshifts had afternoons off and went to see a picture.

Women wanted to pass away their free time because their boy friends or husbands worked late or were in the armed forces.

There was also a special audience for war pictures.

War developments caused a decrease in attendance because of the following reasons:

Many persons had to work longer, had to work at night, made overtime, participated in war activities, and had less time, therefore, for motion pictures.

Some girls and wives attended less frequently because their boy friends or husbands who used to take them worked more or were with the armed forces.

Higher admission made some attend less often.

Increase in night school attendance on the part of young people working in industries.

The situation of formerly unemployed persons who took a job provided a typical example of the same development leading to either more or less frequent motion picture attendance. Some attended more often because they could now afford it; others less often because they had less free time.

Besides these special influences due to the war it was also possible to record some structural changes. They are often of compensating nature.

Children become moviegoers while old people are lost as an audience. Then there is the case of the young housewife whose attendance declines while she has to take care of small children and whose motion picture visits increase again when her children become older and responsibilities fewer.

CHAPTER *8 Some audience preferences*

The audience's likes and dislikes for different types of motion
picture stories have been of concern to producers since the
beginning of the film industry. The importance of the story type
has to be considered in conjunction with the other basic elements of a motion picture. According to various studies made
to ascertain the story type's position relative to other components of a film, it ranks second to the cast in drawing power.[1]
The third component, title, is less influential than the story.
The relative importance of story and title increases whenever
players with low popularity ratings are in the picture.

There are two problems which make it difficult to measure
the relative appeal of different story types. One is the fact that
the story is variable, while the cast and title are stable. The
reason for this is that the story is subject to "treatment." This
refers both to a particular story property considered for a motion
picture, and to story types in general. In this chapter we are concerned with the story type in general. A *western*, for example,
may be a cheap ($100,000) class "B" picture, or it may be an
expensive three-million-dollar production in Technicolor.

[1] See Table 13, p. 36.

Nevertheless, both films come under the heading *western*. The same story type may climb up and down the entire ladder of quality from the highest to the lowest rung. Many moviegoers say, therefore, that they like any kind of story or type of story as long as it is made into a good motion picture.

Another difficulty which has to be borne in mind in this connection is that most motion pictures are not based on any one story type. The majority of them contain ingredients of various story types with a more or less predominant theme. What is actually tested in studies of this kind therefore is this predominant theme rather than a story type.

The ascertaining of audience preferences for story types is, consequently, more difficult than it may appear on the surface. And the results constitute only very general indications for producers, even if they do reflect accurately the stated likes and dislikes of the moviegoing public. The picture type which ranks lowest may be used in a top production with a great cast and an attractive title, and, if skillfully executed, may be an outstanding success at the box office.

According to George Gallup, Audience Research, Inc., has attempted many times to determine whether there is an interest in a specific type of story. It has been found repeatedly that it is the particular story rather than the story type which determines the interest.[2]

The Motion Picture Research Bureau has also attempted to develop techniques to determine general story preferences. An initial difficulty presented itself in the classification of stories. The following list was used in a number of surveys to assist the respondents in deciding their favorite story type.

Classification of Story Types

Comedies:

    Sophisticated comedies
    Slapstick comedies
    Family life comedies
    Musical comedies

[2] Shaw, Robert, "A Package Deal in Film Opinions," *Screen Writer*, March, 1947, p. 35.

War pictures
Mystery, horror pictures
Historicals, biographies
Fantasies
Western pictures
Gangster and G-man pictures
Serious dramas
Love stories, romantic pictures
Socially significant pictures
Adventure, action pictures
Musicals (serious)
Child star pictures
(Wild) animal pictures

This list does not constitute an entirely satisfactory classification due to the overlapping of the different types. A war picture may also be a serious drama, a historical picture, and at the same time it can contain a love story. A socially significant picture may feature a child star. A musical comedy may have the setting of a western picture.

The above breakdown of story types was used for a study conducted in 1942 with two thousand respondents in forty-five towns. The purpose of the survey was to ascertain the likes and dislikes for the story types—or the most popular and least popular predominant themes for motion pictures. The results of the study should be examined in the light of the considerations mentioned before.

Five sets of checklists were used on which the different types appeared in different order to avoid preferences through position. The respondents were first asked to pick out the story types they liked. After they made their choice they were requested to narrow down their selection to the two story types they liked best of all. The same two-step procedure was followed to determine the least popular themes.

Tables 40, 41, and 42 and Chart 6 present the results of this study. Table 40 presents a sex breakdown, Table 41 an age breakdown, and Table 42 an economic breakdown. Each table shows the likes and dislikes for the respective story types. The

RELATIVE STORY PREFERENCES IN MOTION PICTURES
(Based on the Predominant Theme)

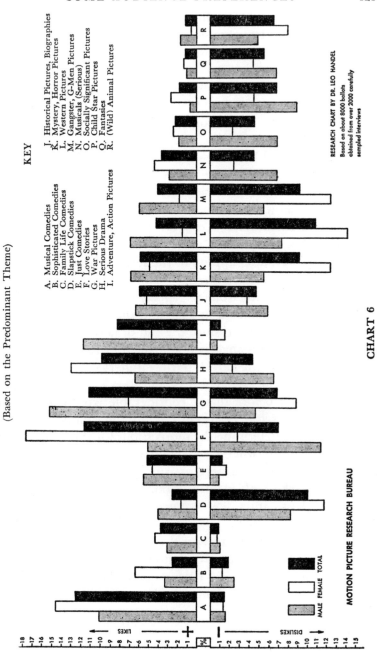

KEY

A. Musical Comedies
B. Sophisticated Comedies
C. Family Life Comedies
D. Slapstick Comedies
E. Just Comedies
F. Love Stories
G. War Pictures
H. Serious Drama
I. Adventure, Action Pictures

J. Historical Pictures, Biographies
K. Mystery, Horror Pictures
L. Western Pictures
M. Gangster, G-Men Pictures
N. Musicals (Serious)
O. Socially Significant Pictures
P. Child Star Pictures
Q. Fantasies
R. (Wild) Animal Pictures

RESEARCH CHART BY DR. LEO HANDEL
Based on about 8000 ballots
obtained from over 2000 carefully
sampled interviews

MALE FEMALE TOTAL

MOTION PICTURE RESEARCH BUREAU

CHART 6

percentages are based on the total mentions in every column. Every one of the two thousand respondents indicated the two story themes he liked best and the two he liked least, resulting in eight thousand statements as the basis for the calculations in the chart and tables mentioned above.

Tables 40, 41, and 42, and Chart 6 show that the comedy complex is well in the lead. For reasons of analysis it had to be broken down into the different types of comedies. This separation made it possible to show that most comedy types are quite popular with the exception of the slapstick comedy. Surveys which do not provide for a separate tabulation of slapstick comedies cannot show significant results.

Romantic themes are extremely popular with women, but rate rather low with men. A similar, if not quite as accentuated, preference differential applies to the serious drama.

War pictures, always a disputed issue, register high with men and much lower with women. It has to be borne in mind that this survey was conducted in 1943 and that the attitude toward war pictures has changed since the end of hostilities.[3] They may be subject to more changes a few years after the war when people begin to forget the hardships they underwent and remember the more enjoyable events of this period.

It was shown before that a considerable part of the female audience dislikes war pictures. The author conducted a study which aimed to determine the motivations for this attitude, and find out especially whether it might be possible to go beyond the anticipated surface reasons, such as aversion to fighting, brutalities, lack of self-identification, unpleasant memories, etc. Eighty-six depth interviews were conducted for this study in New York City in 1949.

Aside from the above reasons the study showed other motivations which counteract potential attendance. First of all, women feel that war pictures, as a rule, confine themselves mainly to fighting, that they lack thorough characterizations of the men

[3] According to a statement of Audience Research, Inc., the interest in war stories decreased only 15 per cent between the time of the height of the war and the beginning of 1947 (Shaw, **Robert,** *op. cit.*).

and therefore human interest drama. Women would prefer a war picture in which the fighting is subordinate to the characterizations of the men who do the fighting. This attitude is probably motivated by the fact that women live with their husbands (fathers, brothers, sons) after the war is over, and that their own lives might be influenced more by the effects of battle than the battle itself.

A thirty-five year old wife of a bank clerk explained her attitude toward war pictures in the following manner:

I feel that there are only very few war pictures which have a real story to tell where the war scenes are only incidental. "Home of the Brave" was a good war picture for me. War pictures made for the sake of showing only fighting awaken unpleasant memories. War is such a repugnant subject showing the stupidity of mankind. In war pictures fighting is made the most important thing, shutting out the real human values, conflicts and emotions. . . .

War films also create in some women a feeling of insecurity. Studies carried out during the war by the Institute of Psychoanalysis in Chicago showed that a woman's fear of loss of her man may increase her emotional dependence upon him. The greater the feeling of dependence, the greater the fear of loss which in turn may result in pathological effects. A woman, unable to identify herself with her husband (boy friend, etc.), can easily regard the Army as her enemy. Associations brought on by war pictures may bring back, consciously or subconsciously, this feeling of insecurity and hence the aversion toward this type of filmfare. Statements recorded during the study such as "I get such an 'uneasy feeling' when I sit through a war picture" fall in this category.

A number of the female respondents stated also that their dislike for war pictures is due to the fact that they stress too much the mechanics of battle and strategy of fighting which they neither understand nor care for. As one young waitress said: "A big tank or bomber gets my boy friend all excited, but it leaves me completely cold."

The comparatively low number of psychological interviews

obtained for this study make a statistical analysis of the returns not advisable. There was, however, a good indication that relatively more women in the lower socio-economical groups than in the higher income brackets want to see war pictures, and also that younger women are somewhat more interested in war pictures than older women. These findings fall in line with the figures shown in the tables.

TABLE 40

STORY PREFERENCES OF MEN AND WOMEN

	Men		Women		Total	
	Likes	*Dislikes*	*Likes*	*Dislikes*	*Likes*	*Dislikes*
Sophisticated comedies	3.3%	2.6%	6.3%	1.2%	4.8%	1.9%
Family life comedies	2.9	1.0	4.2	.7	3.6	.9
Musical comedies	10.0	1.6	14.7	1.4	12.4	1.5
Just comedies	5.5	.8	4.5	1.7	5.0	1.3
Slapstick comedies	3.8	8.3	1.6	11.8	2.5	10.1
War pictures	15.4	4.7	7.1	9.0	11.2	6.9
Mystery, horror pictures	6.8	5.6	4.8	12.7	5.6	9.3
Historicals, biographies	6.3	5.9	5.2	3.8	5.8	4.8
Fantasies	1.0	6.9	1.3	4.5	1.2	5.6
Western pictures	6.9	7.4	1.5	14.4	4.2	11.0
Gangster, G-men pictures	5.8	5.6	1.8	12.7	3.8	9.3
Serious dramas	6.4	6.6	13.2	2.3	9.8	4.4
Love stories, romance	5.0	11.4	18.0	2.7	11.6	7.0
Socially significant pictures	1.8	4.3	2.4	1.7	2.1	3.0
Adventure, action pictures	11.8	.7	4.7	1.5	8.2	1.1
Musicals (serious)	2.7	7.0	4.4	2.4	3.6	4.6
Child star pictures	.6	9.1	2.7	4.5	1.7	6.8
Wild animal pictures	1.6	5.0	.5	8.2	1.1	6.6
No preference	2.0	5.4	1.0	2.7	1.5	3.8
Other	.4	.1	.1	.1	.3	.1
Total	100.0%	100.0%	100.0%	100.0%	100.0%	100.0%

Adventure, western, and gangster pictures register higher with men than women.

Both age and income, as shown in Tables 41 and 42, affect some types of story preferences while they have hardly any effect on others. For example, there is no difference to speak of in the acceptance of musical comedies by moviegoers of different income levels. The serious drama, on the contrary, is very much in demand by higher economic groups while lower income levels show little interest in it. Similarly there is more demand for the serious drama among older people than among younger people, while the acceptance level of the fantasy shows no significant change in the same breakdown.

TABLE 41
STORY PREFERENCES BY AGE

	12–16		17–29		30–44		Over 44		Total	
	Likes	Dislikes	Likes	Dislikes	Likes	Dislikes	Likes	Dislikes	Likes	Dislikes
Sophisticated comedies	2.6%	1.5%	6.3%	1.9%	4.5%	2.0%	3.4%	2.2%	4.8%	1.9%
Family life comedies	3.2	.3	2.2	1.0	5.0	1.1	5.0	.5	3.6	.9
Musical comedies	11.3	2.1	13.1	1.2	13.8	1.4	9.4	1.3	12.4	1.5
Just comedies	6.8	.8	4.5	1.0	4.0	1.6	6.1	2.1	5.0	1.3
Slapstick comedies	4.0	4.4	2.4	10.8	2.9	11.0	1.1	12.6	2.5	10.1
War pictures	13.1	4.4	10.5	7.0	10.5	6.9	11.8	8.9	11.2	6.9
Mystery, horror pictures	8.5	7.6	5.4	8.3	4.5	10.4	5.3	11.3	5.6	9.3
Historicals, biographies	3.8	8.7	5.8	3.7	6.3	4.5	7.1	3.7	5.8	4.8
Fantasies	1.8	5.0	.9	6.4	1.1	5.2	1.3	5.2	1.2	5.6
Western pictures	5.7	12.0	3.6	12.3	3.6	11.1	4.2	7.8	4.2	11.0
Gangster, G-men pictures	4.9	7.8	3.6	8.8	2.8	10.4	4.2	10.0	3.8	9.3
Serious dramas	5.1	6.4	10.3	3.9	10.8	2.9	12.2	5.3	9.8	4.4
Love stories, romance	10.9	11.9	12.6	6.4	12.8	5.5	9.9	6.2	11.6	7.0
Socially significant pictures	1.3	4.9	2.5	3.2	2.2	1.7	2.0	2.4	2.1	3.0
Adventure, action pictures	9.0	.4	9.3	1.3	6.0	1.2	7.1	.9	8.2	1.1
Musicals (serious)	2.4	5.5	3.3	5.3	4.2	3.0	4.1	4.5	3.6	4.6
Child star pictures	2.9	6.7	1.4	8.1	1.5	5.3	2.2	5.9	1.7	6.8
Wild animal pictures	1.5	5.5	.9	5.8	1.3	10.1	.9	4.9	1.1	6.6
No preference	1.2	3.9	1.3	3.6	1.9	4.5	2.4	4.1	1.5	3.8
Other	...	.2	.3	...	.3	.2	.3	.2	.3	.1
Total	100.0%	100.0%	100.0%	100.0%	100.0%	100.0%	100.0%	100.0%	100.0%	100.0%

TABLE 42
STORY PREFERENCES BY INCOME

	High		Upper middle		Lower middle		Low		Total	
	Likes	*Dislikes*	*Likes*	*Dislikes*	*Likes*	*Dislikes*	*Likes*	*Dislikes*	*Likes*	*Dislikes*
Sophisticated comedies	7.5%	.4%	5.5%	1.9%	4.3%	2.6%	2.3%	1.7%	4.8%	1.9%
Family life comedies	3.8	.6	2.7	1.0	3.3	.9	5.2	.9	3.6	.9
Musical comedies	12.1	2.4	14.3	1.2	12.9	1.5	7.9	1.4	12.4	1.5
Just comedies	3.2	1.2	3.6	.9	5.9	1.3	7.8	1.2	5.0	1.3
Slapstick comedies	3.6	13.6	2.8	10.4	2.6	9.3	1.6	7.9	2.5	10.1
War pictures	10.0	7.3	11.5	6.9	11.4	7.3	11.3	5.9	11.2	6.9
Mystery, horror pictures	2.7	11.5	4.9	9.8	6.7	7.9	7.5	9.1	5.6	9.3
Historicals, biographies	10.0	2.1	6.4	4.6	3.9	5.9	4.1	5.7	5.8	4.8
Fantasies	2.0	5.1	1.4	6.4	.8	5.3	.8	5.7	1.2	5.6
Western pictures	2.2	9.2	2.7	12.4	5.3	10.9	6.7	9.1	4.2	11.0
Gangster, G-men pictures	2.4	12.5	2.8	9.2	3.8	8.2	7.5	8.9	3.8	9.3
Serious dramas	13.6	3.5	11.4	4.0	8.7	5.0	5.4	5.9	9.8	4.4
Love stories, romance	9.3	5.3	11.6	6.1	11.6	7.9	13.1	8.4	11.6	7.0
Socially significant pictures	3.7	2.3	2.7	2.9	1.5	2.9	1.1	3.8	2.1	3.0
Adventure, action pictures	7.0	1.0	7.8	1.1	9.7	1.2	7.2	.7	8.2	1.1
Musicals (serious)	3.9	3.5	4.5	4.7	2.8	5.0	3.3	5.9	3.6	4.6
Child star pictures	1.1	7.7	1.0	7.7	2.0	6.7	3.0	4.5	1.7	6.8
Wild animal pictures	1.0	8.8	1.0	5.7	1.0	6.2	1.0	6.2	1.1	6.6
No preference	.8	1.8	.9	3.0	1.6	3.9	2.9	7.1	1.5	3.8
Other	.1	.2	.5	.1	.2	.1	.3	....	.3	.1
Total	100.0%	100.0%	100.0%	100.0%	100.0%	100.0%	100.0%	100.0%	100.0%	100.0%

Several other surveys, by a number of agencies, should be mentioned here even though they do not deal with story preferences in the same manner. One study is aimed at determining the average patron's attitude toward improbable situations and unusual coincidences which can be found in many motion pictures. Another poll analyzes the influence of censorship difficulties on the attendance of a picture. A brief study of how people feel about drinking and smoking on the screen is followed by the perennial dispute of the "double feature." Finally a survey on preferences of newsreel subjects is discussed.

THE PUBLIC'S ATTITUDE TOWARD IMPROBABLE SITUATIONS

The reaction of the audience to "things that can happen only in the movies" is frequently discussed in producer circles and is of concern to many people who work creatively in the making of motion pictures. It seems a timely task to employ a more scientific approach to pin down audience reactions to these occurrences.

TABLE 43

ATTITUDES TOWARD IMPROBABLE HAPPENINGS
IN MOTION PICTURES

Like improbable happenings	51%
Dislike improbable happenings	26
Depends on the type of picture	5
No preference	11
No opinion	7
Total	100%

The investigation in question dealt with improbable rather than impossible happenings and, therefore, did not cover fantasies such as the Topper stories or "Here Comes Mr. Jordan." Depth interviews were used to obtain the answers. Instead of following an exact questionnaire, the investigators first explained the problem carefully to the respondents and then discussed the matter with them freely. About six hundred such interviews with moviegoers were obtained in the New York metropolitan area. The fieldwork was conducted in the spring of 1942.

The over-all results of the study indicate that the majority of people like the improbable occurrences on the screen. A tabulation of the reactions is given in Table 43.

Of the persons in favor of improbable incidents, 20 per cent emphasized that the picture must be good to permit such occurrences. Others stressed that these situations must not be overdone. A number of the respondents expressed their approval of such plots because they make the picture interesting and exciting. Some of them elaborated on the subject by saying that situations of this sort let them "escape" into a world free from the limitations of their own lives.

Almost half the number of persons who were against improbable situations claimed that their opposition came simply from the fact that they had a preference for realistic pictures. Others in the negative group pointed out that these improbable happenings are usually carried too far.

THE PUBLIC'S ATTITUDE TOWARD CENSORSHIP [4]

To determine how much influence censorship has on the moviegoing habits of people, the California Poll questioned a representative group of Californians on what they thought of movie censorship and how they reacted to it.

TABLE 44

QUESTION: DO YOU THINK MOVIE CENSORSHIP IS ABOUT RIGHT, OR IS IT TOO STRICT, OR NOT STRICT ENOUGH?

	Men	Women	Total
About right	47%	46%	46%
Too strict	11	9	10
Not strict enough	26	37	31
No opinion	16	8	13
Total	100%	100%	100%

Most people in California are aware of movies that had censorship difficulties. More than six people in ten say they have heard of movies that have had trouble recently with the censors and could name one or more pictures as evidence.

"The Outlaw" and "Duel in the Sun" were the two movies

[4] The California Poll, Survey Release No. 21, May 24, 1947.

named most frequently as having had trouble with the censors.

Although the biggest group of moviegoers say that a picture's censorship difficulties have no influence on whether they will see the movie, there is a greater number who say they are more likely to see a movie when it has difficulty with the censors than who say they are less likely to see it. More women than men say they are less likely to see a movie when it has trouble with the censors.

TABLE 45

QUESTION: WHEN A MOVIE DOES HAVE TROUBLE WITH THE CENSORS, DOES THAT MAKE YOU MORE LIKELY TO SEE IT, OR LESS LIKELY TO SEE IT?

	Men	Women	Total
No difference	44%	37%	41%
More likely	37	35	36
Less likely	13	25	19
No opinion	6	3	4
Total	100%	100%	100%

Surprisingly enough even those people who do not think censorship is strict enough, do not always stay away from a picture that has had censorship trouble.

TABLE 46

CORRELATION OF CENSORSHIP OPINIONS, ATTENDANCE PREFERENCES

	Movie Censorship is:		
	About right	Too strict	Not strict enough
More likely to see movie	46%	58%	25%
Less likely to see movie	14	15	31
No difference	39	27	39
No opinion	1	..	5
Total	100%	100%	100%

THE PUBLIC'S ATTITUDE TOWARD SMOKING AND DRINKING
IN MOTION PICTURES

The Iowa survey, which covers a cross-section of Iowans over twenty-one years of age, attempted to get a picture of the public's attitude about scenes in films which show men and women drinking liquor and smoking. For this purpose the following questions were put before the moviegoers: [5]

Which one of these three sentences comes closest to your feeling about scenes in the movies which show men and women drinking liquor (smoking)?

(a) I think they are all right the way they are.

(b) I think they are all right in some cases but are overdone in others.

(c) I think they should be left out of movies altogether.

TABLE 47

DRINKING AND SMOKING IN MOTION PICTURES

	Men	Women
Drinking Scenes		
(a) all right as are	19%	16%
(b) sometimes overdone	40	30
(c) should be left out	39	52
No opinion	2	2
	100%	100%
Smoking Scenes		
(a) all right as are	53	31
(b) sometimes overdone	31	26
(c) should be left out	13	40
No opinion	3	3
	100%	100%

An age breakdown showed that movie fans in the twenty-one to thirty age group are much more tolerant of men and women drinking and smoking than are older age groups.

DOUBLE FEATURE VERSUS SINGLE FEATURE

The "double feature" issue became a fierce point of discussion a few years back. Pressure was brought on the industry from individuals and various organizations to change the double feature policy and shift to single feature presentations. The industry countered this demand by pointing out that various experiments in single feature performances resulted in a financial setback to the theater operators involved, who invari-

[5] *Des Moines Sunday Register,* August 31, 1947.

ably lost important business to their competitors. (Deluxe first-run houses and small specialized theaters are not included in this discussion.)

One serious effort to determine where the American public actually stands in this question was made by the American Institute of Public Opinion.[6] The survey, which was conducted in 1940 in all forty-eight states, indicated a moderate over-all preference for the single feature. The subsequent breakdowns show that although 57 per cent of the population prefers single features, there are striking variations between different population groups. Double features are especially popular among persons under eighteen years of age and persons in the lower income groups. The following key question was put before the respondents:

"Would you rather go to a motion picture theater showing a single feature or to one showing a double feature?"

The vote of all groups was 57 per cent for single features, 43 per cent for double features. The most pronounced variations were found in the age breakdown (see Table 48). Also the income groups breakdown shows drastic differences (see Table 49).

TABLE 48
PREFERENCE FOR SINGLE AND DOUBLE FEATURES BY AGE GROUPS

	For single features	For double features
Age groups:		
6 to 12 years	23%	77%
12 to 17 years	42	58
18 to 24 years	60	40
Over 24 years	68	32

TABLE 49
PREFERENCE FOR SINGLE AND DOUBLE FEATURES BY INCOME GROUPS

	For single features	For double features
Income groups:		
Upper	75%	25%
Middle	63	37
Lower	47	53
On relief	42	58

[6] *Motion Picture Herald,* August 10, 1940.

Another indication of the influence of the economic factor is seen in the vote for single and double features according to the price of admission:

	For single features	For double features
Admission:		
Less than 30¢	51%	49%
More than 30¢	67	33

There is little difference in the attitude of the two sexes in the question of double versus single features as the figures indicate below:

	For single features	For double features
Men	56%	44%
Women	58	42

New England was the only section in the country where a majority of the whole population voted in favor of double bills. The attitude of different sections in the country is registered in Table 50.

TABLE 50

PREFERENCE FOR SINGLE AND DOUBLE FEATURES BY SECTIONS OF THE COUNTRY

	For single features	For double features
New England states	43%	57%
Middle Atlantic states	55	45
East Central states	62	38
West Central states	57	43
South	58	42
Rocky Mountain states	62	38
Pacific Coast states	56	44

The reasons most frequently given by those opposing double bills in order of importance are: (1) that one or both of the features are likely to be a "poor" picture; (2) that sitting through a double feature is fatiguing and takes too much time; (3) that seeing two full-length pictures is confusing because, as one woman puts it, "you generally think about a picture when you get home and a double feature gets you mixed up."

Those who like double features give as their chief reasons: (1) that a double bill gives moviegoers more for their money; (2)

if one picture is inferior, the other is likely to be good and in any event adds variety; and (3) a double feature gives those who attend a chance to "kill more time."

While the survey indicated that a majority of the American public prefers single features, a more thorough examination of the records shows that it would not be right to say that double features as such are directly responsible for keeping many persons away from the box-office. The reasons go deeper. The adverse vote on double bills is more a reaction to "poor" pictures often found as the "lower half" of the double bill, than to the fatigue and time involved in seeing a double bill. Persons interviewed who disliked double features were asked whether they would change their attitude if both pictures on a double bill were good. When this qualification was added, opinions divided 64 to 36 in favor of double features.

Although many respondents complained that double features are too long, only 10 per cent apply the remedy of walking out when the second feature comes on. The remainder stay to "get their money's worth."

As mentioned before, industry experiences do not bear out the results of this survey. Whenever exhibitors have changed from a double to a single feature policy, their business has declined. The RKO theater circuit tried to play single features in their New England houses but had to abandon this policy in favor of double features. As one spokesman of this organization put it, "This was forced upon us, even though we tried to stem the adoption of the double bill." Loew's chief case in point is the Ziegfeld Theater in New York where single features were tried and resulted in a marked loss of attendance until this policy was revoked.

The seeming contradiction between the survey and the actual experiences of the industry might be explained partly by the sample used by the American Institute of Public Opinion and partly by the background of the problem. The cross-section canvassed was a representative sample of the population of the United States over six years of age. It was not a cross-section of moviegoers. There is a difference between these two groups. A cross-section of the motion picture audience contains, for instance, a greater representation among the younger age groups than does a straight national sample. Though the cross-section used for this survey was not made known to the author, it is assumed that the younger people were not represented in proportion of their frequency of motion picture attendance. Yet the survey points out that younger people up to seventeen years of age are in favor of the double bill.

The presentation of the results of this survey eliminated also the group of respondents who were "undecided" or who didn't know whether they preferred singles or doubles. This omission might also be responsible for the fact that the difference between the two groups appears as large as it does. For purposes of analysis and evaluation, the inclusion of this group would have been of interest.

Another circumstance that should be considered was that the single bill adherents were responsible for much public discussion of this issue before this survey. The answers of many respondents might have been influenced by this publicity. Some might have said they favored single features while in fact they preferred double bills whenever there was an alternative—it just may have seemed smarter and more sophisticated at this time to favor single bills. Such assumptions become stronger when we realize that it requires only a little attention to schedule one's movie visit so that the unwanted second feature need not be viewed.

TABLE 51

QUESTION: WHAT KIND OF PROGRAM DO YOU PREFER?

Program compositions:

Two features with newsreel and short	46%
One long film with newsreel, short, and organ solo	20
Two features with newsreel and organ solo	33
Don't know	1
Total	**100%**

A survey conducted in Great Britain also tried to determine the public's preference in program composition. The question was included in the Bernstein film questionnaire of 1946–47, and the study was conducted among the patrons of the Granada theater chain in London. Many motion picture experts feel that this survey gives a very good indication of the actual attitude toward the problem, and the results might also come very close to the preferences of moviegoers in the United States. In Table 52 we find only a fifth of the respondents indicating a clear preference for single features.

PREFERENCE FOR NEWSREEL SUBJECTS

Preferences for the various subjects covered in newsreels can be measured without difficulty. One study pertaining to newsreel content was conducted by the Motion Picture Research Bureau in the summer of 1942. Preferences for newsreel items change with time. This survey was conducted early in the war and the large majority of patrons indicated a great interest in war shots. Detailed results of the study are presented in Table 52.

TABLE 52 [1]

PREFERENCE FOR NEWSREEL ITEMS			
	Men	Women	Total
Newsreel subjects:			
War news	89%	81%	85%
Sports events	20	4	13
Fashions	..	13	7
National domestic affairs	2	2	2
Other miscellaneous subjects	1	1	1
No preference	4	8	6
Do not care for newsreels	1	3	2

[1] Due to multiple mentions, percentages add up to more than 100.

The analysis is based on the responses of 516 persons questioned in the New York area. As usual, the survey covered moviegoers only and there was an attempt to obtain a well balanced cross-section.

Most of the persons who gave war news as their preference had no specific type of war news in mind. A number of respondents, however, specified certain topics, such as naval activities, war production, particular war theaters (especially the Russian front), aviation news, bombing raids on the enemy, activities of

the American soldiers at home and abroad, and defense preparations in the United States. About half of the interviewees who
mentioned these specific aspects of the war had some personal
interest in the subject, such as a son in the Navy, or a husband in
a war plant.

Sports events ranked second, due to the large interest of males
and the younger age groups, and fashions third, due to the preference expressed by younger women.

It can be safely assumed that newsreel items other than war
shots became increasingly important after the end of hostilities.
The breakdown in Table 52 is, therefore, mainly of historical
value.

CHAPTER 9 *Audience preferences for players*

Two types of research studies are employed to measure the popularity of motion picture actors and actresses. One constitutes a general star rating which is periodically established and which shows some similarity to the Hooper ratings for radio programs. The other method covers studies which are conducted for specific players when a producer requires special information about them.

GENERAL STAR RATINGS

Stars and players represent a considerable investment for the company to which they are under contract. There are expenditures such as the salaries paid for a number of years (many of the well known movie actors earn between $100,000 and $200,-000 a year), costs for the buildup while the "star is made," and general publicity for the player which is continuously disseminated by the studio, in addition to specific publicity for the motion pictures the star appears in.

The popularity of motion picture players and any increase or decrease in their popularity are matters of great concern to the company to which they belong, to the actors themselves, to their agents, and to many other persons active in production, distribution, and exhibition.

As outlined previously, the industry uses various methods, as fan mail analysis and box-office studies to obtain a picture of the popularity of players. It has been pointed out that these methods do not satisfy the most primary tests of reliability. Star ratings are a more scientific way of determining the popularity standing of motion picture players. They attempt to provide the following information:

(a) Relative popularity rating of the players covered by the study at the time of the survey.

(b) Popularity trend of players over a period of time which is especially important for relative newcomers.

(c) Effect of different pictures on the player's popularity. This serves as an indication of the kinds of parts in which the audience likes or dislikes the player.

(d) Special sex, age, social, and geographical breakdowns to determine audience likes and dislikes of various strata.

The indexes can be established in different ways. One method used by the Motion Picture Research Bureau is based on the same principle as the one used for picture ratings.[1] The interviewees are shown the name of a star and asked to indicate their degree of interest with the aid of a checklist. The different evaluations may range from "Star X is my favorite movie star," to "I dislike Star X very much." Each of the different evaluations corresponds to a certain appeal index rating, ranging from 100 to zero. The average computed from the different reactions is the popularity index.

Another method expresses the popularity index in terms of "want-to-see." The question put before the respondents would be formulated somewhat along these lines:

If you knew nothing about a movie except that Player X appeared in it, would you want to see it?

The proportion of affirmative answers obtained to this question is the basis for the popularity index. Audience Research, Inc., makes extensive use of this method.

Chart 7 shows an example of the popularity trend of a motion

[1] See Audience Appeal Index, p. 67.

picture star, and provides information about the way in which different pictures affect the popularity of a player. The index jumps from 60 to 80 after the release of Picture I. However, it drops after the release of Picture II. The hypothesis is that the audience liked the player in the part he played in the first pic-

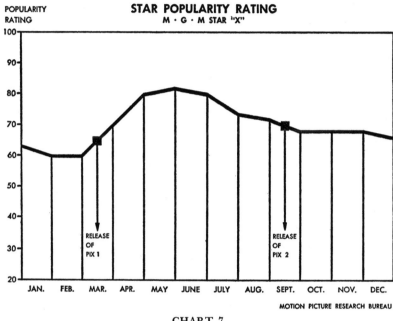

POPULARITY
RATING

STAR POPULARITY RATING
M · G · M STAR "X"

RELEASE
OF
PIX 1

RELEASE
OF
PIX 2

JAN. FEB. MAR. APR. MAY JUNE JULY AUG. SEPT. OCT. NOV. DEC.

MOTION PICTURE RESEARCH BUREAU

CHART 7

ture, but felt that he was miscast in the following production. The same chart also indicates that popularity slowly declines when a star is not seen in a picture for some time.

Audience Research, Inc., has made a significant contribution to star ratings by providing breakdowns of the total ratings according to sex, age, income, and frequency of attendance. With such information the film producer can avoid combining stars whose following comes from the same stratum of the audience, and can compose a cast which will appeal to many different sections. If one star is especially liked by younger people, for instance, an effort may be made to co-star him with another player who has a following among older people. According to Gallup's organization, an adding up of players who are admired by the same section of the audience would not draw appreciably more people to the box-office.

STUDIES FOR PARTICULAR PLAYERS

It was noted before that general star ratings sometimes need to be complemented by special studies pertaining to specific players. The necessity for special research studies with regard to individual actors may arise from various other reasons.

Two types of studies are outstanding in this field:

(a) Studies pertaining to new or potential motion picture stars, to determine how they are being received by the audience.

(b) Studies covering well-established players who are believed to be losing their popularity or whose decrease of popularity is indicated by the general star rating.

As in the case of star popularity ratings, it is also important for these special studies to provide for the various audience breakdowns to discover the likes and dislikes of various sections of the moviegoing public.

For example, a survey was carried out to find to what extent, and why, the popularity of a prominent motion picture star was declining. A checklist was employed providing for key answers which were to be followed up with a probing "why?" question. The name of the player who was under analysis has to be withheld for obvious reasons. For our purpose he will be called "Star X."

The persons questioned had seen Star X at least once before the survey was conducted. They were handed the checklist and asked which of the statements contained therein, if any, would come close to their own feeling about this player. The checklist contained these five statements:

(a) Star X is my favorite movie star.
(b) Star X is one of my favorite movie stars.
(c) I like Star X, but I don't like him as much as I used to.
(d) I don't like Star X, but I used to like him sometime ago.
(e) I never cared for Star X.

The key statements of this checklist were obviously statements (c) and (d), because the survey aimed to reach the segment of moviegoers whose interest in this player had waned.

The number of mentions of the two key statements made it possible to estimate the degree of decline of the popularity of Star X. The responses to the "why?" question obtained from respondents who checked statements (c) or (d) was of even greater importance, as they indicated clearly the reasons behind the figures obtained.

Here are typical comments obtained from respondents who indicated through the medium of checklists that their interest in certain movie stars had declined.

A young salesgirl commented about a well-known actor as follows: "I used to like Star X very much when he was playing in important supporting roles. Now that he is playing leads he is not as attractive to me as he used to be. Somehow he can't keep up my interest in the part he portrays."

A college student about a young actress: "I don't care for this actress any more because Hollywood is trying to make a singer out of her, but she definitely can not sing. I preferred her in previous pictures where she did not have to sing."

A housewife about an actor who used to play the lead as the son in family pictures. "Star X used to be one of my favorite stars. However, now he is definitely getting too old for the juvenile characters he is playing. He should have more adult parts. I am sure he would do an excellent job because he is one of our best actors, however badly miscast at the present time."

THE MARGARET O'BRIEN STUDY

To illustrate the type of study that may be conducted to test the potential star value of a newcomer to the screen, we cite the following study of Margaret O'Brien.[2]

This star was introduced to the moviegoing public in 1942. The first picture in which she was featured, with Robert Young and Laraine Day, was "Journey for Margaret." Next she appeared in a trailer, "You, John Jones," with James Cagney and

[2] Permission was obtained from Metro-Goldwyn-Mayer to publish the findings of this study.

Ann Sothern, in which she recited the Gettysburg Address. The purpose of the trailer was to promote the idea of civilian defense.

Fan mail to the studio and a preview survey conducted before the release of "Journey for Margaret," plus other indications, showed that moviegoers who had seen Margaret O'Brien had become very interested in her and wished to see her again.

TABLE 53

QUESTION: WHO IS YOUR FAVORITE CHILD MOVIE PLAYER UNDER
TWELVE YEARS OF AGE?

	Men	Women	Total
Margaret O'Brien	9%	14%	12%
Roddy McDowall	10	8	9
Baby Sandy	3	5	4
Larry Simms	3	3	3
Carolyn Lee	2	3	2
Butch Dudley	1	2	1
Billy Severn	1	1	1
Others	5	7	6
I have none, don't know	66	57	62
Total	100%	100%	100%

Producers with Metro-Goldwyn-Mayer were anxious to know whether Margaret O'Brien could carry a leading part. To get a better picture of the potential star value of this new player, a survey was conducted early in 1943, with the following objectives:

It had to be determined how many moviegoers knew about Margaret O'Brien at this time; how her popularity compared with that of other child players; and how people who had actually seen her on the screen evaluated her. The most important question aimed to ascertain the potential star value of this newcomer, or to determine the proportion of moviegoers who, having seen Margaret O'Brien, would go to see a picture in which she played a leading part.

The fieldwork for this study covered about fourteen hundred interviews with moviegoers which were obtained in twenty-two towns across the country.

The questionnaire first of all attempted to establish Margaret

O'Brien's popularity relative to other child players. Table 53 shows the results obtained by this question.

The returns were tabulated in three groups. Respondents who had seen Margaret O'Brien were divided into those who had seen her in either "Journey for Margaret," or the trailer, "You, John Jones," and those who saw her in both productions. The results broken down in this manner revealed clearly the cumulative effect of multiple exposure. The answers to the second key questions are shown in Table 54.

TABLE 54

QUESTION: FROM WHAT YOU HAVE SEEN OF MARGARET O'BRIEN WHICH OF THE FOLLOWING STATEMENTS COMES NEAREST TO YOUR RATING:

Margaret O'Brien is	Saw "You, John Jones" only			Saw "Journey for Margaret" only			Saw both		
	Men	Women	Total	Men	Women	Total	Men	Women	Total
a) the best child movie player I have ever seen	10%	12%	11%	16%	26%	21%	17%	30%	24%
b) one of the best child movie players I know	32	38	35	44	47	46	55	56	56
c) a good child movie player	53	42	48	36	25	30	26	14	19
d) just a fair child movie player	3	5	4	4	1	2	2	...	1
e) not a good child movie player	...	...	...	...	...	...	...	...	...
No answer, don't know	2	3	2	...	1	1	...	...	...
Total	100%	100%	100%	100%	100%	100%	100%	100%	100%

The answers to the third key question show Margaret O'Brien's star potentiality in decisive terms (Table 55).

TABLE 55

QUESTION: IF YOU KNEW NOTHING ABOUT A PICTURE EXCEPT THAT MARGARET O'BRIEN PLAYED THE LEADING PART, WOULD YOU GO TO SEE IT?

	Saw "You, John Jones" only			Saw "Journey for Margaret" only			Saw both		
	Men	Women	Total	Men	Women	Total	Men	Women	Total
Yes	50%	55%	53%	57%	73%	65%	57%	81%	70%
No	31	22	26	26	16	21	34	12	22
Don't know	19	23	21	17	11	14	9	7	8
Total	100%	100%	100%	100%	100%	100%	100%	100%	100%

The outcome of a survey conducted in January, 1946, may be of interest in this connection. The same question, "Who is your favorite child movie star?" was put before a cross-section of moviegoers and answered as in Table 56.

TABLE 56

WHO IS YOUR FAVORITE CHILD MOVIE STAR?

	Men	Women	Total
Margaret O'Brien	53%	60%	57%
"Butch" Jenkins	6	7	6
Peggy Ann Garner	3	5	4
Roddy McDowall	2	2	2
Other	6	5	6
No favorite child star	30	21	25
Total	100%	100%	100%

The increased popularity that had been predicted in the 1943 study was borne out in fact.

THE DRAWING POWER OF MALE AND FEMALE STARS FOR MOVIEGOERS OF THEIR OWN SEX

Various film studies have indicated that male audiences frequently prefer male to female stars, and that female patrons prefer female to male stars. Similar observations have also been made in magazine and radio research.

Lazarsfeld, in the report mentioned before,[3] finds that "the favorite movie star of the average woman is an actress, not an actor," just as "Westerns are most popular in the Rocky Mountains," and as old people like movies with older heroes. In all preference studies, Lazarsfeld suggests we find a strong element of projection, a phenomenon which is best documented in studies of magazine readership, but which seems to prevail in the other mass media as well.

This theory has also been proclaimed by Mayer,[4] who tells us that "It is quite common for the dreamer, male or female, to imagine himself or herself in the place of the hero or heroine of the particular film."

[3] Paul F. Lazarsfeld, "Audience Research in the Movie Field."
[4] Mayer, J. P., *Sociology of Film*, p. 153.

Also *Time* magazine, reporting on surveys conducted by Gallup, says, "The No. 1 box-office draw is Spencer Tracy. The next 13 favorites with boys and men are all males . . . the fourteen favorites of women are evenly split between male and female stars. But women generally go to the pictures to see women. . . . Most movie-goers are inclined to bestow their greatest affection upon stars of their own sex. . . ." [5]

Another survey conducted by the Granada Theatres, Ltd., among fifty thousand London children from seven to fifteen years of age, showed that girls place women characters high on their list, while women fall to the bottom of the boys' list. [6]

To determine the extent and nature of this phenomenon, a study was conducted by the Motion Picture Research Bureau in 1947 in New York City. One hundred depth interviews were recorded by a trained psychologist. Only respondents who attended motion pictures at least once a month were covered in the study, their interest for male or female stars being determined by the introductory question: "Who are your favorite movie stars?" Respondents who mentioned only players of their own sex or who mentioned a majority of players of their own sex were subjected to the detailed interrogation.

The tabulation revealed that 65 per cent of the respondents showed a preference for stars of their own sex. That is more apparent with men than with women. Seventy-six per cent of the men showed more interest in male stars, while 54 per cent of the women showed more interest in female stars.

The reasons for the moviegoer's preference for players of their own sex can usually be traced to "self-identification," ranging from conscious and obvious self-identification to motivations related only remotely to this phenomenon. Table 57 shows a classification of the answers.

Conscious self-identification

This attitude was found more frequently in men than in women. It is a frank admission by the moviegoers that they step

[5] *Time,* July 21, 1941.
[6] *The Bernstein Children's Film Questionnaire,* Report, 1947, p. 3.

out of their limited world to live for a few hours the lives of their screen favorites. Men, therefore, identify themselves with the men on the screen, and women put themselves in the position of the film actresses.

There exists also an indirect form of identification. Parents, in some instances, identify their children with the players on the screen. As Thorp put it, "The woman who has abandoned

TABLE 57

REASONS FOR PREFERENCE OF STARS OF OWN SEX

	Number of Mentions [1]
1. Conscious self-identification	35
2. Emotional affinity	27
3. Own sex better acting ability	22
4. Idealization, idolization	10
5. Admiration of fashion, styles	4

[1] Some respondents mentioned more than one reason.

all hope of any glamorous existence of her own can still escape reality by identifying her offspring with the happy creatures that flit across the screen." [7] Statements such as "I like June Allyson because she reminds me of my own child" are encountered frequently.

The following condensed statements of respondents who are part of the category of conscious and obvious self-identification:

As far as I'm concerned there are many wonderful female stars but it is easier for me to put myself in the place of a male actor and understand and appreciate his portrayal. This I believe is more important than the admiration felt for a female star.

(Male, age group 18–29, copy writer)

He plays roles which could happen to any man, you get a picture of yourself. These players are the screen version of what a man would like to be. (Male, age group 30–44, Army captain)

When watching the screen I probably watch the women more, but in picking my favorite I'll pick my own hero, that is a person who typifies the things I'd like to be. (Male, age group 18–29, salesman)

[7] Thorp, *America at the Movies*, p. 78.

They are smart, capable actresses, they live their parts. They make you feel that the roles they act are real, as if they were living it and so they draw you into the story and make you feel as if you were part of it.   (Female, age group 18–29, nurse)

Like the characters they portray on the screen. The reason for men liking men is that they try to picture themselves in their place, can't do that with a female star.
                          (Male, age group 18–29, furniture finisher)

Every woman desires to have the qualities of their favorite stars, naturally a woman can't pick a man as her favorite. I admire these stars and would like to be like them.
                          (Female, age group 30–44, secretary)

These actresses I mentioned are great. They make me feel every emotion of their parts. I feel as if it were myself on the screen experiencing what they do.   (Female, age group 30–44, saleswoman)

Emotional affinity

Emotional affinity is closely related to the above form of self-identification. It is, however, not always recognizable as such on the surface. The difference in the emotional make-up between the sexes seems to cause a greater interest in players of one's own sex than the opposite sex. Men usually represent action, power, and movement, while women usually play emotional parts. The psychological structure of the man in the audience comes closer to that of the man than the woman on the screen, and vice versa. The moviegoer is, therefore, more interested in the problems, and reactions of his counterpart on the screen. He asks himself how he would handle the situations he sees portrayed.

Emotional affinity is more frequently encountered in women than in men. Here are a few statements of interviewees to elaborate on the above statement:

It's easier and more natural for a man to understand and appreciate a male actor's part.   (Male, age group 18–29, unemployed)

Like male actors better, their parts make place for more action and adventure, things a man might do himself. Believe men as a whole prefer action to emotion, while women prefer emotion to action. Therefore, men prefer male stars, and women female stars.

(Male, age group 30–44, baker)

Picked for dramatic abilities, think as a whole women have more dramatic ability than men. Definitely prefer emotional, dramatic pictures to action, adventure pictures. When Davis and Colbert play their parts you feel that you yourself could be living it, it makes you very emotional. I think to myself: "This could happen to me."

(Female, age group 18–29, student)

Their acting abilities, their personalities, their imaginations are outstanding. Prefer pictures with dramatic backgrounds to action pictures. When watching Hepburn and Bergman you get lost in the part yourself.   (Female, age group 30–44, secretary)

Own sex better acting ability

Some moviegoers, especially men, think that players of their own sex have better acting ability. The "sticking up" for their own sex is in the final analysis also a form of self-substitution, even though a rather remote derivation.

In this connection it may be interesting to note that men chose a much larger variety of stars as their favorites than women. While men mentioned twenty different players more than twice, women gave only nine stars more than two mentions. Men chose mainly the "he-man" types while the majority of women concentrated on Ingrid Bergman, Bette Davis, and Greer Garson, actresses mostly representing purely emotional parts.

The belief that their own sex has better acting capabilities can be seen from the following statements:

The male actor has to be taken on his merit. The female can ride on glamour. Prefer acting to looks. Believe that the male star brings something on the screen which men would like to be or do.

(Male, age group 18–29, contractor)

Portrayals are natural and real. True to life. Generally consider male actors better than female, the women can be aided by clothes, and makeup, etc.

(Male, age group 18–29, assistant cafeteria manager)

These actors have adventurous parts to play. I don't like emotional pictures and roles. I think the men are much better actors than the women. (Male, age group 18–29, student)

They are good character actresses, think the men are mostly terrible. Like the parts they play, prefer a good dramatic piece to an action story. (Female, age group 30–44, salesgirl)

Think majority of females are better actresses than men are actors. Women are more emotional than men, like emotional roles better, as portrayed by women on screen. A good emotional actress makes you feel as if you were living her part yourself.

(Female, age group 30–44, housewife-photographer)

Idealization, idolization

This is an attitude which was most frequently encountered with younger, female moviegoers. They single out one or more movie stars for their special attention. The admiration is actually the link to imitation which in turn connects again with self-identification. Also in this case it is logical that you can imitate only a person of your own sex. Again, a few actual comments:

Like the way they act, like the parts they portray, admire their personalities, not so much their looks.

(Female, age group 30–44, nurse)

Think they are the kind of people I would like to know, or even be like. I admire them. (Female, age group 12–17, student)

A woman pictures herself in their place. Admire them and would like to be like them. (Female, age group 18–29, dress shop manager)

Most women are not too imaginative. They like to have someone to "be like," therefore, they choose someone of their own sex. Favorites play mature roles. Women must have someone to emulate, styles, certain characteristics.   (Female, age group 18–29, secretary)

Bergman is different and Crawford is wonderfully sophisticated and both have great dramatic ability. When looking at them, especially Bergman, there is a sort of idolization. I would like to be like her.
                    (Female, age group 18–29, college student)

Admiration of fashion, styles

This is a well known manifestation which is responsible for the fact that Hollywod fashions find acceptance all over the nation and beyond the borders of the United States. Obviously, there are mainly younger women in this group. Imitation is again a form of self-identification.

The available material in this field suggests the conclusion that motion picture players may be typed according to four main groups, and that the composition of their following reflects the type these players usually represent on the screen. Male stars are usually of the "he-man" or the "romantic" type. Humphrey Bogart and Alan Ladd are examples of the first designation, and their following is relatively higher among men than among women. The prime example of the "romantic" was Rudolph Valentino, and a contemporary example is Peter Lawford—who is liked mainly by young girls. Female players can be divided into the "emotional" and the "glamour girl" types. Bette Davis exemplifies the "emotional" type, and we find among her fans more women than men. But Betty Grable, because of the roles usually assigned her, is often considered America's typical glamour girl; and as such she appeals relatively more to men than to women. Her rather artificial roles seem to make it difficult for female moviegoers to identify themselves with this actress.

This study and the deductions made from it do not exhaust the investigations that could be carried on in this field; rather, they suggest an interesting area of research for social psychologists. The results might well be used by the producer who wants to increase the potential audience for a film by combining, in one picture, players appealing to different audience sectors.

THE SELECTIVITY OF THE AUDIENCE

In discussion of audience preferences for story types and picture players, we cannot overlook a general difference in approach to the choice of filmfare on the part of the attendants. Moviegoers can be divided in a general way, according to the manner in which they select motion pictures, into selective and nonselective patrons.

There are different degrees of selectivity. A selective patron may be one who plans to see a certain picture on a certain date in a certain theater. He may also be a person who walks through the theater district with the intention of seeing just any picture and there makes up his mind whether he should see the picture in theater A or the one in theater B.

A selective moviegoer can generally be described as a person who as a rule uses some degree of discrimination in choosing motion pictures, and selects them prior to the time of attendance.

Many persons are sometimes selective and sometimes not, according to the pictures available and according to circumstances.

The selective moviegoers particularly are the target of advertising and publicity designed to influence their choice in favor of a specific product. The nonselective audience is exposed to the same media, with the aim of making it positively selective for the product being promoted.

The proportion of these two groups has been subject to a number of inquiries. But audience selectivity remains a challenge for more intricate research studies, as only a little concrete information has been obtained in this field so far. According to Audience Research, Inc., there are 5,400,000 people in America who go to see practically every picture regardless of what is playing, but 70 per cent of the people who go up to the box-office to buy a ticket know what picture they are going to see before they come to the theater. On the other hand, more than one-fourth of all moviegoers buy tickets without knowing anything about the feature but its title.[8]

[8] *Time,* July 22, 1946, p. 94.

One survey of the Motion Picture Research Bureau in which the question came up was conducted in New York in 1941.[9] The survey was conducted for another purpose, but the following question was asked:

Last time you went to the movies did you a) just want to see any picture, b) wish to see this particular show, or c) go because somebody else suggested it?

The respondents answered as follows:

Any picture	49%
This particular show	36
Because somebody else suggested it	12
Other reasons	3
Total	100%

According to these figures almost half of the moviegoers questioned admitted that they were nonselective. No further effort was made to analyze the degree of selectivity employed by the 36 per cent who admitted they had intended to see a particular show. There is some bias in this form of questioning, since it is quite possible that some respondents may not wish to admit their indifference for filmfare.

The question of selectivity was again taken up in connection with a survey conducted in 1943. While the first study was based on street and house-to-house interviews, the respondents of the second study were interviewed before and after their attendance in ten different theaters in the New York metropolitan area. Most of these theaters showed different pictures, but all were major productions supported by promotional campaigns. Here again the survey was not primarily concerned with the selectivity of moviegoers, and the questions pertaining to it had to be limited. The following question was put before the 2,700 moviegoers questioned in the survey:

When you decided to go to the movies today, did you intend to see ———— (pictures running at the theater where the interview took place) or did you just want to go to the movies?

9 Handel, Leo, *Studies of the Motion Picture Audience.*

Current picture	49%
Any picture	51
Total	100%

"Any picture" (51 per cent compares well with the results of the first survey (49 per cent). In the second study there was an attempt, however, to get a more accurate picture of the degree of selectivity exercised by the respondents. The persons who mentioned that they had come to see the current picture were further questioned as follows:

If it had not been possible for you to see this picture today, would you have gone to the movies anyway?

No	21%
Yes	23
Don't know	5
Total	49%

The percentages above are based on the total number of respondents. It shows that great discrimination was actually only used by 21 per cent of the moviegoers. It is possible that even this low percentage is still inflated due to bias in this issue.

TABLE 58

SELECTIVITY BY INCOME GROUPS

	High	Middle	Low
Just movies	36%	52%	59%
This particular show	44	34	31
Because somebody else suggested it	15	11	8
Other reasons	5	3	2
Total	100%	100%	100%

An analysis of the figures shows an interesting trend in the income groups breakdowns. Table 58, taken from the 1941 study, shows that higher income classes exercise a much higher degree of selectivity than lower socio-economic groups.

The lower degree of selectivity of the low income group may be traced to the fact that this segment of the population is generally not as well informed as persons on the higher socio-economic levels. That ties in with Knupfer's findings [10] to the effect that public opinion surveys give a good deal of evidence that the "low status" group on the whole shows less interest in news of any kind than the "high status" group.

The attendance frequency of the selective audience is lower than of the indiscriminating moviegoers. The relationship is similar to radio listening habits, where the relationship between selectivity and quantity is also negative and unlike reading habits where the identical relationship is positive.[11]

[10] Knupfer, Genevieve, "Portrait of the Underdog," *Public Opinion Quarterly*, Spring, 1947, p. 109.
[11] Lazarsfeld, P. F., *Radio and the Printed Page*, p. 185.

CHAPTER **10** *The film in relation to other media of mass communication*

Many observers in the field of communications feel that the different mass media—motion pictures, newspapers, and magazines—compete for their audiences. They believe that a good radio show cuts down the box-office returns of the neighborhood cinema, and that a good newscaster conjured to the bedside by a twist of the wrist affects the turnover of the newsstand on the corner.

That there is some competition between the different communications media cannot be denied. But the results of a series of research studies conducted by different organizations, at different places and at different times, throw another light on this matter. According to these inquiries there is a positive correlation between radio listening, motion picture attendance, and newsreading.[1] The people who see movies are also apt to listen to the radio and read newspapers frequently.

The results of some studies show that the communications media actually stimulate interest in each other. The radio listener sometimes buys a newspaper to get a more detailed account of an event he heard mentioned on a newscast. Every day thou-

[1] Handel, Leo, "Radio, Movies, Publications Increase Each Other's Audience," *Printers' Ink*, July 19, 1946.

sands of film fans buy a paper for the single purpose of looking up a movie program. A newspaper reader sees a review of a motion picture and wants to see that picture. The story of an outstanding motion picture may be published in a book, in a magazine or in a newspaper, or may be heard as a radio serial. A film commentator on the radio may cause a listener to see a motion picture he recommends.

But this mutual stimulation does not seem to be the only cause of the positive correlation among the audiences exposed to the various media of communication. Apparently the ardent radio fan is the same type of person who would show a considerable interest in motion pictures and current news events, whether they concern the UN or the problems of Li'l Abner.

The advertising field quickly recognized this situation. Motion picture advertising in newspapers is an old and established routine. The advertising of selected radio programs in newspapers and magazines seems to be gaining ground. Motion picture advertisers are using air time on an increasing scale. The advertising of newspapers over the air, which started some years ago, has proved its value.

The following figures show the results of some research studies which established the positive correlation in question, expressed in terms of frequencies. In most instances the data obtained were merely part of a larger complex under investigation.

The figures obtained are, with one exception, purely quantitative. They merely compare the amount of time or frequency of movie attendance, radio listening or reading, and give part of the answer that is wanted. But they point toward a vast and interesting program of research that should aim for qualitative evaluation: to determine, for example, what types of motion pictures the listeners of certain types of radio programs prefer, and what types of news they turn to in their publications for this information.

The first of the studies under discussion compares radio listening with the attendance of motion pictures. The survey was conducted by the Motion Picture Research Bureau in 1941, for the Office of Radio Research (now Bureau of Applied Social Research).[2] Over five hundred interviews were conducted in the New York metropolitan area and the analysis of the results shows clearly that persons who do not listen or rarely listen to the radio attend the movies less frequently than persons who listen to the radio a great deal.

Radio listening during the evening in hours	Average monthly movie attendance
0	2.5
0 to 1	3.1
1 to 2	4.0
2 to 3	4.2
3 to 4	3.9
over 4	4.5

Movie and radio audiences were also compared in a study conducted by Dr. F. L. Whan of the University of Wichita.[3] The survey covered the state of Iowa, where 9,218 interviews were conducted by students from Iowa State College in March and April, 1942.

Table 59 shows the number of hours spent each day listening to the radio according to frequency of movie attendance.

TABLE 59

CORRELATION OF MOVIE ATTENDANCE AND RADIO LISTENING

	Monthly attendance of the movies		
	Over 1	1	0
Hours spent listening to radio:		*Men*	
Per weekday	3.79	3.32	3.25
During morning	.76	.64	.68
During afternoon	.99	.87	.98
During evening	2.04	1.81	1.69
		Women	
Per weekday	4.88	4.58	3.98
During morning	1.17	1.16	1.07
During afternoon	1.55	1.42	1.46
During evening	2.16	2.00	1.45

We see again from this that the radio listening increases with attendance at movies. The correlation appears to be most marked between evening radio listening and movie attendance.

[2] Handel, Leo, *Studies of the Motion Picture Audience.*
[3] Whan, F. L., and Summers, H. B., *The 1942 Iowa Radio Audience Survey.*

The persons covered by the Whan study in Iowa were also asked whether they took a daily newspaper and how many magazines they read during the thirty days preceding the interview. Table 60 shows the relationship between newspaper and magazine reading, and the time spent listening to the radio. The respondents are arbitrarily classed as follows: Those who do not read a daily newspaper are called "Nonreaders"; those taking a daily newspaper and reading fewer than four magazines a month are classed as "Semi-readers"; and those taking a daily newspaper and reading more than four magazines per month are called "Readers." The table shows that the more a person reads newspapers and magazines the more time he also spends listening to the radio.

TABLE 60

CORRELATION OF RADIO LISTENING AND READING

	Men			Women		
	Reader	Semi-reader	Non-reader	Reader	Semi-reader	Non-reader
Hours spent listening to radio						
Per weekday	3.86	3.40	3.27	4.81	4.55	4.09
During morning	.75	.68	.65	1.16	1.10	1.09
During afternoon	1.07	.93	.98	1.47	1.41	1.39
During evening	2.03	1.79	1.64	2.18	2.04	1.61

The relationship of newspaper reading and news listening was also investigated by Frederick J. Meine in his paper "Radio and the Press Among Young People." [4] Meine interviewed 1,200 junior and senior high school students in Trenton, New Jersey, in 1940. His qualitative analysis differentiates between "serious" and "nonserious" reading. The following newspaper features were classified as "serious" items: foreign news, local and state political events, editorials, national politics, columnists, and book reviews.

According to Table 61, over 70 per cent of those who are good newspaper readers listen to the radio news at least once a

[4] Lazarsfeld, Paul F., and Stanton, Frank, *Radio Research, 1941* (New York: 1941).

day. Almost the same proportion of frequent news listeners also are frequent and serious newspaper readers. Conversely, only about 45 per cent of the students who have either poor radio or newspaper habits are good news consumers in the other medium.

TABLE 61

RELATIONSHIP BETWEEN RADIO NEWS LISTENING AND NEWSPAPER READING

| | Radio news listening | | |
	Once a day	Less than once a day	Total
Frequency and type of newspaper reading:			
Read newspaper at least once a day and read "serious" items	496	208	704
Read newspaper less than once a day and/or read no "serious" items	219	277	496
Total	715	485	1200

The positive interrelation that we find between movie and radio exposure, and between radio listening and reading, exists necessarily also between movie attendance and reading. The following table is from a recent study by Lazarsfeld and Kendall based on a cross-sectional sample.[5]

TABLE 62

RELATIONSHIP BETWEEN BOOK READING AND MOVIE ATTENDANCE

Movies seen during previous month:	Do not read books	Read books
No movies	44%	26%
1 to 3 movies	35	43
4 or more movies	21	31
Total	100%	100%

As we would expect, the book readers go to movies far more frequently than those who do not read books.

The foregoing studies give evidence of the fact that the same people who expose themselves to one medium are apt to expose themselves to others as well, but from such evidence we are still not able to determine whether it is the actual influence of one

[5] Lazarsfeld, P. F., and Kendall, P. L., *Radio Listening in America* (New York: Prentice-Hall, Inc., 1948).

form of communication or exposure to another, or whether, on the contrary, it is merely a result of the fact that certain types of individuals are simply more active in their communication habits than other individuals. A few studies support the first hypothesis.

The inter-stimulation of books and films was indicated in a study conducted by the American Institute of Public Opinion.[6] In 1937 and again in 1938 the Institute made a survey asking a cross-section of persons, "What is the most interesting book you have ever read?" The tabulated answers ran like this:

1937

The Bible
Gone with the Wind
Anthony Adverse
The Good Earth
Magnificent Obsession
The Green Light
Les Miserables
Ben Hur
David Copperfield
The Count of Monte Cristo
Little Women
Drums Along the Mohawk
American Doctor's Odyssey
Treasure Island
How to Win Friends and Influence People
Uncle Tom's Cabin
All Quiet on the Western Front
The Virginian
Adventures of Tom Sawyer

1938

The Bible
Gone with the Wind
Anthony Adverse
The Citadel
How to Win Friends and Influence People

[6] Thorp, *America at the Movies*, p. 243.

The Good Earth
Ben Hur
Northwest Passage
Little Women
A Tale of Two Cities
Les Miserables
Magnificent Obsession
Adventures of Tom Sawyer
Treasure Island
The Count of Monte Cristo
Robinson Crusoe
Ivanhoe
The Green Light
David Copperfield
Call of the Wild

Nearly all these books have been seized upon by Hollywood as motion picture material, and even the Bible has been screened in part. *Anthony Adverse* was brought to the screen and became one of the leading "money" films of 1935. *The Citadel, The Good Earth, Little Women, Northwest Passage,* and *A Tale of Two Cities* have been turned into outstanding pictures. *Ben Hur,* seventh on the list, was one of the greatest box-office pictures of all time.

What film treatment may mean to the life of a book is indicated by the fact that merely to break even a good picture must show to about fifteen million persons. A book, on the other hand, can become a bestseller if it sells a few thousand copies. Hollywood did not create the original popularity of these books, but in giving them film treatment and a far greater audience the movies have unquestionably added to the circulation and endurance of the books themselves.[7]

Thorp lists a few concrete examples of how motion pictures stimulated the reading of books. The appearance for instance of "Lives of a Bengal Lancer" will sweep public library shelves of ever book on India. "The Barretts of Wimpole Street" emptied Cleveland shelves for months, not only of every biography of the Brownings but of every poem of Elizabeth Barrett and the

[7] *Ibid.,* p. 246.

poems of Robert Browning. When "The Good Earth" was shown in Cleveland, even the Braille copies of this book were in constant use while the film was shown.

Thorp points out that the idea of making the library a source of telephone information about films playing in local theater originated in Macon, Georgia, was copied by the public library in Los Angeles, and is now nationwide. A call to the library in many cities will give you not only the names of all the films showing in local playhouses but information about cast, director, suitability for youthful audiences, book source, or historical period.

Books made into screen stories gain popularity through the medium of motion pictures. And films, in turn, stimulate the reading of the books they are based on.

TABLE 63

TIME SPENT IN READING AND COMPETING ACTIVITIES

Activities "yesterday"	Per cent of 4,000 persons	Average minutes per person	Total hours	Per cent of total hours
Read book	21%	13	877	8%
Read newspaper	85	35	2,367	21
Listened to radio	74	85	5,683	49
Read magazine	40	19	1,280	11
Went to movies	12	18	1,225	11
Total			11,432	100%

The relative amount of time spent in reading, radio listening, and motion picture attendance was the object of a study conducted by the Psychological Corporation.[8] The bureau made a detailed survey of book reading and buying habits in 1945, and questioned a cross-section of four thousand persons for this purpose. The questions we are concerned with in this context covered newspaper reading, magazine reading, book reading, radio listening, and motion picture attendance on the day before the interview. The interviewing was spread proportionately over the various days of the week. Therefore, taking "yesterday" as a base, valid comparisons of the time spent on the five activities

[8] Link, H. C., and Hopf, H. A., *People and Books.*

may be drawn. Table 63 shows the time spent in reading and competing activities. The figures show that radio listening is first by a wide margin, followed by newspaper reading. The time spent on motion picture attendance is eighteen minutes per day or just over two hours a week.

Another analysis made by Lazarsfeld and Field [9] tried, among other things, to determine the preference for newspaper reading, radio listening, and motion picture attendance. For this purpose the following two questions were put to 2,571 respondents.

Question: If you had to give up either going to the movies or listening to the radio, which one would you give up?

Movies	84%
Radio	11
Don't know	5
Total	100% = 2,246

Question: If you had to give up either reading the newspaper or listening to the radio, which one would you give up?

Newspapers	62%
Radio	30
Don't know	8
Total	100%

Another question in the same study had the purpose of determining how the public evaluated the part played by magazines, newspapers, radio, and motion pictures in public service during the war.

Question: Taking everything into consideration, which one of these do you think did the best job of serving the public during the war—magazines, newspapers, moving pictures, or radio broadcasting?

Magazines	3%
Newspapers	17
Moving pictures	4
Radio broadcasting	67
No opinion	9
Total	100%

[9] Lazarsfeld, P. F., and Field, Harry, *The People Look at Radio* (Chapel Hill, N. C.: University of North Carolina Press, 1946).

On all counts, radio appears to receive the highest evaluation of all the media. Movies, on the other hand, appear near the botton of the scale, both in time spent in attendance and in importance to people. This is probably explained by several factors. Movies are relatively expensive. They require more effort on the part of the individual to get to them, and they are more explicitly for the purpose of entertainment, so that they could more easily be dispensed with.

Television, a powerful new medium of mass communication, recently has come into existence. The impact of television on the motion picture industry in general, and on theater attendance in particular, is by necessity an undecided issue. One can hardly anticipate the eventual influence of a medium while it is in the process of establishing itself. Furthermore, most published studies covering the relation of motion picture attendance and television viewing show a rather unsatisfactory research procedure or an insufficient sampling. Whether the positive correlation observed between other important mass media will finally hold true in the case of television and motion picture attendance cannot be conjectured at this time.

CHAPTER 11 *Content analysis of movies*

Content analysis [1] of any medium of communication generally serves one of two functions. It may constitute the basis of a sociological study to determine what cultural patterns and stereotypes are reinforced in a given medium or in a given segment of a medium, or it may be used as the first step in an "effects" study. Systematic procedures for content analysis of the various media have been developed by Lasswell, Leites, and others,[2] and many studies of this kind (of printed material especially) have been made.

The first type of content analysis is a major research undertaking itself, and may comprise analyses of settings, plots, characters, symbols, or any other specific attribute of content. Thus the motion picture producer or sociologist who wanted to know to what

[1] This chapter on content analysis is taken largely from Fiske, Marjorie, and Handel, Leo, "Content and Audience Analysis," *The Journal of Marketing*, October, 1946.

[2] Lasswell, H. D., "A Provisional Classification of Symbol Data," *Psychiatry*, I (May, 1938), 194–207; *Analyzing the Content of Mass Communication: A Brief Introduction* (Washington, D. C.: Library of Congress, Experimental Division for Study of War Time Communications, Document no. 11, 1942). Also Leites, N. C., and Pool, Ithiel de Sola, *On Content Analysis* (Washington, D. C.: Library of Congress, Experimental Division for Study of War Time Communications, Document no. 26, 1942). For a summary of the literature see Berelson, B., and Lazarsfeld, P. F., *The Analysis of Communication Content* (Bureau of Applied Social Research, Columbia University, forthcoming).

extent current films actually reflect current American life would subject a representative sample of films to an elaborate quantitative analysis, counting and classifying plots, settings, characters, symbols, goals, methods, and so on.

Magazine fiction, to cite one example from another field, has been analyzed in this way to determine the nature and extent of the portrayal of racial stereotypes.[3]

In a study of motion pictures by Wolfenstein and Leites,[4] a psychological pattern of the general population was shown as represented in the treatment of the heroine on the American screen. The "good-bad girl" of the movie, who turns out to be pure in the end but who appears in the early sequences as forward or promiscuous, results, according to the authors, from the ambivalence of the American male toward the opposite sex. The good girl is demanded as a marriage partner, but at the same time the bad girl is thought to be more rewarding sexually. In a large number of movies, Hollywood provides a happy solution by combining the two.

Another variation of this same general type of study involves not the detection of basic cultural or psychological themes, but of propaganda themes. After the war a number of studies were done to discover what appeals were made by German propaganda movies and how they were made.[5]

There have been few content analyses of motion pictures from any of these standpoints, but there are three worthy of note here: The work of Dorothy Jones[6] and the work of Dale[7] and Peters[8] in the Payne Fund Studies. More recently a type of

[3] Berelson, B., and Saeter, P., "Majority and Minority Americans: An Analysis of Magazine Fiction," *Public Opinion Quarterly*, Summer, 1946.

[4] Wolfenstein, Martha, and Leites, Nathan, "An Analysis of Themes and Plots," *Annals of the American Academy of Political and Social Science*, November, 1947.

[5] See Kracauer, Siegfried, *Propaganda and the Nazi War Film* (New York: Museum of Modern Art Film Library, 1942). For a discussion of such studies see Lazarsfeld, P. F., and Merton, R. K., "Studies in Radio and Film Propaganda," *Transactions of the New York Academy of Sciences*, Vol. 6 (1943), No. 2.

[6] Jones, Dorothy, "Quantitative Analysis of Motion Picture Content," *Public Opinion Quarterly*, Fall, 1942, pp. 411–28.

[7] Dale, Edgar, *The Content of Motion Pictures* (New York: Macmillan, 1935).

[8] Peters, C. C., *Motion Pictures and Standards of Morality* (New York: Macmillan, 1933).

content analysis was developed by the Motion Picture Research Bureau, which will be described later in this chapter.

Dale was concerned both with methodology and with securing a general classification of motion picture content. He conducted analyses of three different intensities. The first consisted of virtually the entire product of feature films from the major producers for the years 1920, 1925, and 1930. Five hundred pictures for each of these years were classified according to the following major themes:

> Crime
> Sex
> Love
> Mystery
> War
> Children
> History
> Exploration
> Comedy
> Social propaganda

The classification was determined through the reading of reviews.

The second level analyses covered 115 pictures. These films were viewed at the theater by observers and reported by means of a special schedule. Each observer read a review before attending the theater. He recorded pertinent comments at the theater and wrote the complete report immediately after viewing the film, classifying the content of the movie according to the following categories.

SOCIAL VALUES OF MOTION PICTURES:
(1) Nature of American life and characters
(2) Nature of foreign life and characters
(3) Motivation of characters
(4) Emotional appeals to the audiences and methods of making them
(5) Crime, delinquency and violence
(6) Relations of sexes
(7) Military situations

(8) Depiction of underprivileged peoples
(9) Deportment, language, manner of tone and voice, type of dialogue and songs

A more intensive analysis was then performed on forty of the selected films. A dialogue from each script was obtained from the producer. The observers familiarized themselves with the scripts before attending the picture, took stenographic notes on points not covered by the script while viewing the film, and wrote up the report in running narrative form.

The result was an impressive array of statistics on the amount of love, crime, drinking, and brutality portrayed, and information on the sort of goals preferred by the heroes and heroines.

Dale's approach, however, was primarily moralistic and his analysis schedule was based on "values" or "detriments" which were in turn based on favorable and unfavorable criticisms of motion pictures.

The same approach also characterizes another Payne Fund Study which endeavored to relate content to the mores, to see whether the movies reflect or distort the approved mode of conduct. It was, in other words, a comparative analysis involving some content analysis, rather than a content analysis *per se*.

This study was made by Peters,[9] who selected scenes from 242 pictures representing varying degrees of "badness" of conduct as rated by various groups of judges. The scenes selected related to treatment of children by parent, lovemaking, and democratic attitudes. They were then shown to selected groups (such as faculty, college students, business men, factory workers, and so on) who were asked to rate them according to "goodness" or "badness."

Peters used the following method. Each member of the sample received a package containing a number of concretely described bits of conduct taken from motion picture situations which were to be classified as follows:

Admire very much
Approve

[9] *Ibid.*

Neutral (conduct taken as a matter of
course, behavior okay)
Disapprove
Disapprove very much

Peters concludes on the basis of these classifications that some scenes are admired and others disapproved among all groups, but "in the matter of aggressive lovemaking by girls, the conduct depicted in the movies is distinctly below the approved standards of every group studied."

Dorothy Jones, another person who has worked extensively in this field, differs from Dale in two respects. In the first place, she was not "concerned with devising methods for evaluating whether films are 'good' or 'bad' or for recommending what films should or should not contain." She has been interested solely in recording, summarizing, and analyzing what is presented on the screen. The second difference between the Dale and the Jones studies is a methodological one pertaining to the use of scripts. Dale had the observers read the script before viewing the picture to acquire a frame of reference, whereas Mrs. Jones felt that a "fresh reaction to the screen presentation was essential to an accurate analysis of content." Unfortunately those methods have not been compared experimentally, so it is not possible to evaluate them.

Neither study purports to be infallible from a scientific viewpoint. The published account of the Dale investigation does not include a detailed description of methodology, and raises many questions as to procedure, terminology, etc. The Jones study, according to Mrs. Jones herself, was weak from two standpoints. In the first place, the reliability of the schedules used have not been conclusively demonstrated, and second, no attempt was made to obtain a representative sampling of the product. Both studies reveal a certain lopsidedness in the screen's portrayals of life, but because of the inadequacy of the sampling in the one study and the unclear methodology in the other, it is clear that definitive descriptive work is yet to be done in this field.

Another variation of the first main variety of content analysis is illustrated in Table 64, which indicates how newsreels have

TABLE 64

TEN YEARS OF NEWSREEL ANALYSIS [1]

1939–48

	1939	1940	1941	1942	1943	1944	1945	1946	1947	1948
National news:										
Aviation	3.1%	.8%	.9%	.1%	.2%	.4%	1.4%	3.2%	1.8%	1.7%
Disaster, fires, etc.	3.4	3.1	2.6	2.3	1.4	1.7	1.9	3.0	4.0	2.1
Farm	.2	.4	.2	.6	.7	.2	.2	.5	.4	.4
Fashions, styles	1.8	1.6	1.5	.9	.5	1.0	.9	1.5	1.2	2.3
Governmental news	5.1	4.5	5.8	8.6	7.8	2.7	11.7	8.4	8.2	6.2
Health	.4	.4	.2	.1	.6	.9	.1	.6	.4	...[4]
Industrial progress	.7	.9	.6	.1	1.0	.3	.3	.5	.1	.3
Labor news	.8	.1	1.5	.3	.7	.3	.8	2.4	1.3	1.0
National defense	4.1	13.7	24.7 [2]	23.3 [2]	22.2 [2]	13.3 [2]	3.4 [2]	7.1	4.3	4.5
Political news	.8	7.3	.1	.1	.3	5.0	.1	.6	.3	6.1
Religious news	1.0	.6	.7	.4	1.0	1.5	.8	2.3	.8	1.0
Science	1.1	.2	.3	.1	.2	.2	.9	.7	.5	.7
Sports	26.1	25.0	26.2	15.3	8.6	9.1	9.4	18.3	26.2	23.1
Weather	.8	1.1	.4	.4	.2	.6	.3	.5	.9	.5
Miscellaneous	21.8	15.9	12.9	15.1	8.9	9.2	20.3	17.2	18.1	18.2
Foreign news	18.3 [3]	5.8 [3]	4.2 [3]	2.9 [3]	2.1 [3]	1.4 [3]	23.7 [3]	29.7	29.3	30.3
War in Europe	10.5	18.6	15.8	15.0	28.9	37.7	9.7	...	...	...
War in Pacific	...	...	1.4	14.4	14.7	14.5	14.1	...	...	...
United Nations	...	...	...	...	...	...	...	3.5	2.2	1.6
	100.0%	100.0%	100.0%	100.0%	100.0%	100.0%	100.0%	100.0%	100.0%	100.0%
Total "clips"	4,940	4,947	4,948	4,454	3,810	3,491	3,133	3,559	3,484	3,541

[1] Compiled from Movietone News, News of the Day, Paramount News, Pathe News (Warner Pathe News, after August 15, 1947) and Universal Newsreel.
[2] Including domestic war activities after United States' entry into World War II.
[3] Excluding World War II coverage.
[4] Less than .1%.

represented historical trends in their proportionment of topics. The war, for instance, is clearly reflected in the large amount of attention given to war news and national defense views between 1941 and 1944. Continuing studies of this sort may in the future provide an informative index of the amount of concern for various topics in different eras.

The second kind of content analysis, that which constitutes the first step in a study of the effects of particular motion pictures, has been limited largely to small investigations made under government or educational auspices. Examples are those done by the Bureau of Applied Social Research on indoctrination films for the War Department, and on a documentary war film for the British Ministry of Information. As a preliminary step in studying effects, these films were witnessed several times by trained observers to determine what factors might influence audience reaction, what natural sections it falls into, what scenes have aspects which might "boomerang," or produce an effect contrary to the one expected, and so on.

Thus the preliminary content analysis of a documentary film designed to show the complexity of the problems involved in the reconstruction of occupied territory revealed that there were several sequences which might theoretically produce reactions not at all connected with the main theme. For example, among many other shots showing the physical reconstruction of the city, there was a very brief one showing Negro engineers at work. This scene was not described as such in the script, and without the prior analysis of the film the investigators might well have overlooked a shot which proved to have a marked effect on particular segments of the population.

The Motion Picture Research Bureau developed a content analysis chart which covers many important aspects of a film, permits a relatively fast recording of the subject matter as well as a speedy analysis. This chart was designed so that the information to be recorded can be punched on IBM cards. The basic layout of the analysis chart is shown in Table 65. The main classifications can be seen next to the IBM card column numbers 1 to 65. Due to the lack of space the subclassifications within the columns were not listed, however, their divisions can be easily conjectured. For example, column 25 "Marital status and changes of lead A" is subdivided into some of the following groups:

x   single throughout picture
y   married throughout picture
0   widowed
1   divorced
2   single at beginning, married during picture
3   married at beginning of picture, divorced during picture
4   married during picture and widowed during picture

In addition to the information transcribed on the IBM cards every picture covered by the analysis is listed also on a general index card which contains information such as title, IBM code number of picture, players, producing company, director, producer, etc.

Content analysis of motion pictures is in the pioneer stage, and there is still much challenging work to be done in the development of techniques. At the present time they are very time-consuming because several trained observers must witness a film several times, recording their observations by hand during and/or after viewing the film, and re-checking them.

A few experiments checking results based on one viewing with those based on several viewings of the film, however, might reveal that for some purposes one viewing by two observers would suffice. Similar tests with scripts and films might be made to determine whether certain items (simple counts of the sex or nationality distribution of major and minor characters, for example) could not be analyzed from the scripts alone.

Content analyses done so far are concerned mainly with characters or plot types. Further work in this field might indicate the practical value of analyzing settings, type, and duration of photographic shots, degrees of physical and psychological realism, and so on.

From the standpoint of the social scientist, no picture of contemporary culture will be complete until the content of this

TABLE 65

CONTENT ANALYSIS CHART

Coded for use of IBM Cards

Column	x	y	0	1	2	3	4	5	6	7	8	9

Column	Description
1–4	Code number of picture
5	Country of origin
6	Screening time in five minute time segments
7	Color process
8–9	Main story type
10–12	Secondary story elements (36 classifications)
13	Time period at beginning of picture
14	Time interval covered by picture
15	Geographical designation
16–18	Sociological designation and changes in status of leads A, B, and C
19–21	Age of leads A, B, and C at beginning of picture
22–24	Race, religion, leads A, B, and C
25–27	Marital status and changes of leads A, B, and C
28–30	Sex of leads A, B, and C
31	Children in picture
32	Importance of part and characterization of professional persons
33	" " " " " " business men
34	" " " " " " public officials
35	" " " " " " politicians
36	" " " " " " religious workers
37	" " " " " " races or nationals
38	" " " " " " unskilled labor
39	" " " " " " armed forces personnel
40–41	Sports (type and prominence)
42–43	Dancing (type and prominence)
44	Place of drinking liquor
45	Amount of drinking
46	Brutality
47	Type of crime(s)
48	Fate of criminal(s)
49	Smoking of principal characters
50–51	Sex (lovemaking, prominence)
52–53	Music (type of and prominence)
54	Gambling, result of gambling
55	Physical deformities
56	Religious ceremonies (denomination, prominence, treatment)
57	Court scenes (prominence, treatment)
58	Fashions (prominence)
59	Trademarks
60–61	Technical procedures (including medical, scientific processes, etc.)
62	Educational value
63	Entertainment value
64	Critics reactions
65	Relaxation value

most popular of all mass media has been subjected to systematic and continuing scrutiny. From the standpoint of the producers, no criticism about the lack of representativeness of the Hollywood product can be adequately met until they know to what extent a sampling of their films actually reflect or distort "real" life.

CHAPTER **12** *The effect of the movies*

Most of the empirical work on the effect of motion pictures has not been done by commercial firms working for the film industry, but by educational groups, interested in movies either as a social force motivating the attitudes and behavior of young people or as a teaching device along with other recently developed visual aids in education. The series of investigations going under the name of the Payne Fund Studies,[1] for instance, was subsidized by an educational foundation and constitutes practically the only attempt so far to gain insight into movies' social effects. "Experimental" work in educational effects has been conducted mainly in classrooms by various teachers' colleges. So we are dealing here mainly with studies conducted on a typical audience, composed of children and young people in college; but since our interest is in methods rather than results, this fact should not be disturbing.

In speaking of the effects of films on the audience, we are apt to be referring to a variety of different things. The *unit* which we presume is having an effect may vary. It may be the movies in general that are under discussion, and studies may be con-

[1] Twelve studies and a summary, under the general direction of W. W. Charters, published in nine volumes by Macmillan.

ducted to trace the over-all effects of the medium. At other times it may be a certain type of film—the crime picture or the love picture—that is under investigation; or it may be a single production or even a particular scene in a production. Finally the unit may consist of a film in combination with some other element—such as a preliminary lecture, as in the case of many educational film experiments.

There is another dimension that needs to be considered—the *nature* of the presumed effect. Movies, or a type of movie, or a single film might be studied to discover the effect on some broad social matter such as crime and delinquency, or the general level of morality of the community, or other long-range changes in people's attitudes. But investigations may also be aimed at much more specific types of effects—such as the acquisition and retention of factual knowledge. Again movies may be studied in respect to the needs they fulfill for various types of individuals; or we may be interested only in persons' immediate reaction to films in terms of emotional response or in terms of "like" and "dislike."

For whatever purpose the effects of movies are studied, there are certain methodological problems common to all cause-and-effect studies, that must be dealt with. An investigator must establish, for instance, that the group presumably affected by a movie or by movies actually has been exposed to the unit in question. He must show that a change (effect) has really taken place in their attitudes or behavior. He must prove that the observed change has taken place as a result of the movie or movies and not because of some other factor that may have been operative at the same time. These requirements seem rather obvious, but they create difficulties in the design of effect studies that have never been entirely overcome, though they may be partly circumvented in closely controlled experiments. In the discussion which follows we will see how the investigators have met the problem of establishing cause-and-effect relationships between movies and the behavior and attitudes of people.

We shall treat the studies here according to the sort of effect the investigator is examining. Studies dealing with broad social effects—particularly the Payne Fund Studies—will be examined first, followed by a survey of experiments on the use of films in education, and then a discussion of studies which are concerned with the immediate reaction of audiences to film content. In the last part of the chapter we shall discuss briefly some of the highly specialized studies conducted by the Research Branch of the United States Army during World War II.

SOCIAL EFFECTS OF MOVIES

One of the Payne Fund Studies, Blumer's *Movies and Conduct*,[2] represents an early attempt to explore the effect of motion pictures on the behavior and attitudes of children and young adults. Blumer obtained his material for this study through a rather diffuse approach, gathering evidence from many sources at once. Some 1,800 "autobiographies," were collected, over half from among college students and most of the remainder from high school students. These were reports especially written for the study and were attempts by the students to trace the effect of movies on their own actions and ideas. Another source was over one hundred detailed interviews which covered the same area. In a third method, volunteer investigators, usually members of college fraternities and sororities, participated in conversations concerning movies, and later recorded the various statements. Grade school students were investigated through still another technique—direct questionnaires—of which about twelve hundred were distributed and collected. Finally, the behavior of children as they watched motion pictures and as they played afterwards was observed.

From information gathered in this variety of methods, Blumer was able to come to several general conclusions; that children imitate the action of movie stars, that movies are apt to produce heightened emotions of fear, sorrow, and passion, but at the same time may produce an opposite reaction of detachment and boredom, and that movies may produce for certain children a whole new, and perhaps false, view of the world.

This was, explicitly, an exploratory study designed to gain in-

[2] Blumer, Herbert, *Movies and Conduct* (New York: Macmillan, 1933).

sight into the effects of movies rather than clearly to designate the direction and extent of such effects. The sample was in any case not representative of American youth, being composed of a very disproportionate number of college students. For this reason there is very little information on the different roles which movies play in the lives of different groups of children. We have no way of knowing, for instance, in what ways the children who are terrified by scenes in motion pictures differ from those who are detached or scornful of them.

The author might have been more specific about the nature of the contribution which his various research techniques made to the finished product. Did the autobiographies elicit more information than the interviews? At several points he indicates that the findings of one technique were corroborated by another, but it is difficult to tell, generally, at what points one or another of the methods proved the most useful.

Another study of the Payne Fund series, *Movies, Delinquency, and Crime* [3] has three rather more specific aims—"to consider (1) the role of motion pictures in the lives of delinquents and criminals of both sexes; (2) the effects on the inmates of motion pictures shown at correctional schools, reformatories, and penitentiaries; and (3) some effects of crime pictures on non-delinquent boys and girls." For the first problem some seven hundred interviews, and life-histories were obtained with assorted young criminals and delinquents. A large amount of questionnaire material was obtained from the inmates of various penal institutions, and, for the third question on effects among nondelinquents, some of the life-histories gathered for *Movies and Conduct* were used.

The authors were not able to reach very definite conclusions as to the effect of movies on crime. They do say that they are a "factor of importance" in the lives of some criminals, and that on the whole "motion pictures have relatively little reformation value." But it would be impossible to conclude from the results that movies produce more crime than they prevent or even that

[3] Blumer, Herbert, and Houser, Philip M., *Movies, Delinquency, and Crime* (New York: Macmillan, 1933).

an individual's reaction to movies is of a causative nature rather than a result of previous conditioning toward criminal activity.

This study, as in the case of *Movies and Conduct,* is "uncontrolled." There is no attempt to test young peoples' attitudes on behavior *before* and *after* movie experiences to see what changes have taken place. Nor is a sample of moviegoers compared with non-moviegoers to see what differences occur in their criminal behavior, nor a sample of criminals with non-criminals to see what differences occur in their reaction to movies. The whole validity of both these studies depends on the respondent's ability to trace their own actions back to motion pictures. In the final analysis, the subjects themselves are made the judges of the determinants of their behavior.

In a study by Shuttleworth and May,[4] however, an attempt has been made to approximate a controlled experiments by matching a group of moviegoers under observation with a group of non-moviegoers, or persons who go to the movies less frequently, on the theory that the differences in attitudes or behavior between the two groups would be attributable to the effect of movies.

The subjects of this study were some fourteen hundred students of several New England high schools, selected on the basis of a questionnaire concerning frequency of attendance at motion pictures. Only the 10 or 15 per cent who were most avid moviegoers and the 10 or 15 per cent who attended the least frequently were selected. The two groups were matched in respect to background characteristics and intelligence.

The moviegoers and non-moviegoers were contrasted on the basis of a large number of criteria. Teachers were asked to rate each individual according to his scholastic average, his deportment, and various character traits. Fellow students also rated their popularity, and a series of "reputation" scores were derived. The students were given a large number of "objective tests of conduct"—tests of honesty, self-control, etc. The second part of the study was concerned with the attitudes of the two

[4] Shuttleworth, Frank K., and May, Mark A., *The Social Conduct and Attitudes of Movie Fans* (New York: Macmillan, 1933).

groups of children toward a wide range of factors, from nationality groups to prohibition.

In 90 per cent of the comparisons made between the two groups, there were no significant differences observed. Where differences did occur, the non-moviegoing children generally received the most "favorable" scores. They rated higher in the various facets of deportment and reputation. The moviegoers, on the other hand, were more apt to be chosen as friends. In respect to attitudes, there occassionally appeared significant differences. The moviegoing children tended to value smart clothing much more highly, for instance; and when asked which they would rather be, a movie actor or a college professor, 69 per cent of the non-moviegoing children chose the professor, and only 47 per cent of the moviegoers.

The main difficulty with the approach used in this study, as the authors themselves point out, is that we have no way of determining whether the differences observed actually result from movie attendance or from some prior cause that itself determines moviegoing. The children who admire smart clothing, for instance, might be of a type more likely to attend movies, and their attitude toward clothes would not be a result of their movie habit but equally with it a symptom of their personalities. We might even argue that movie attendance is the *result* of some of the attitude factors measured.

The three studies discussed so far have one factor in common. That is, that they have attempted to discover the cumulative effect of motion pictures, rather than the effect of a single film or the effect of movie experiences over only a limited period of time. There is much to be said for such an approach. Any single motion picture could be studied experimentally—that is, through the actual introduction of the stimulus (movie) to a selected group of subjects. But such an experiment suffers from the limitation imposed by the fact that generally only one movie can be tested, and the effect of a single production is circumscribed by the total effects of other productions. As May and Shuttleworth point out, an anti-Chinese film may be balanced by a pro-Chinese film. Or two pro-Chinese films could have an effect, while either alone would have none. If we wish to discover the over-all social effects of movies we cannot do so atomistically by studying single productions. This is tantamount to saying that it is extremely difficult to do so experimentally.

The experimental method, however, has the tremendous advantage of making more sure that the observed "effect" is the result of the movie or movies in question and not of some other factor. Occasionally, too, experiments may be extended over a considerable length of time so that we can at least approximate an evaluation of cumulative effects.

Peterson and Thurstone,[5] in studying attitude changes among school children brought about by motion pictures, employed what has been called the "successional" experimental method. They examined their subjects before and after viewing the motion pictures which the investigators selected. The subjects themselves, therefore, acted as the control group in the premovie examination. Later we shall see examples of "simultaneous" experiments in which one group (the experimental group) is shown the film (or films) which is withheld from the others (the control group.)

The authors here were interested in a fairly wide range of attitude changes, in attitudes toward war and crime, toward various nationality groups and toward capital punishment, gambling, and prohibition. They selected commercial films which bore upon these points, and arranged to give their experimental group free tickets to these films when they appeared in the local theaters. Before the movie, the students were given either a scaled attitude test, or a paired comparison schedule which was repeated some weeks later—just after the movie had been seen.

In some cases the respondents were tested again after a period of several months to see if the attitude change had persisted. In a few experiments, also, Peterson and Thurstone attempted to obtain the cumulative effect of movies by testing the students

[5] Peterson, Ruth C., Thurstone, L. L., *Motion Pictures and the Social Attitudes of Children* (New York: Macmillan, 1933).

before and after seeing a group of two or three movies on the same subject.

The general findings were that the movies *did* have an effect upon attitudes. "The Birth of a Nation," for instance, tended to create considerably more anti-Negro sentiment than had existed before. The effect of the movies persisted also, even after a considerable period of time, although there was some tendency to return to the pre-movie attitudes. In respect to the cumulative effect of several movies, it was discovered that two or more films, each of which does not produce any noticeable changes when seen alone, may produce such changes when seen in succession.

The advance in methodology of this study over the others reported before is obvious. The authors here have been able to observe actual changes, while in the other cases the investigation could only infer that changes had taken place. Even in this case, however, there is not exactly an airtight control of all factors, *besides* the movies in question, that might have brought about the observed changes. We do not know what else the subjects did during the period of two or more weeks between the two tests, and so we can never be certain that other factors might not have been influential. A more rigid control could have been imposed if in each case another group, which did not see the movie, was tested in the same period, and any changes occurring in their attitudes compared with the changes among the experimental group.

A more recent study by Rosenthal[6] is of interest, for it attempted to eliminate this inadequacy. The purpose of Rosenthal's investigation was "to measure the influence of extreme radical labor motion picture newsreels upon socio-economic attitudes (a) in general (b) upon attitudes the content of which is closely related to the theme of the pictures (c) upon attitudes the content of which is not directly related to the theme of the picture." The subjects were undergraduate students in several psychology courses.

[6] Rosenthal, S. P., *Changes in Socio-economic Attitudes under Radical Motion Picture Propaganda.*

The experimental group was given attitude tests before and after viewing the movies, just as in the case of Thurstone's experiments, and the differences were measured. But a control group, also, was given the tests and *not* exposed to the movies, to see what changes might have occurred without the introduction of the stimulus. A much more precise measure of control was thus obtained. The results are in line with expectations— that radical motion pictures do produce significant differences in attitude, and that attitude differences are more marked in regard to attitudes directly connected with the subject matter of the film than with peripheral attitudes. One interesting finding, however, was that in regard to certain attitudes movies may have just the opposite effect from that anticipated by the propagandist. The students were asked to score their degree of agreement or disagreement with the statement that "radicals are enemies to security." They tended, actually, to agree with this statement more *after* viewing the films. Such boomerang responses have been discovered elsewhere in communication effects. We will discuss them in a subsequent chapter.

One final study might be mentioned in connection with the social effect of movies, Wiese and Cole's "A Study of Children's Attitudes and the Influence of a Commercial Motion Picture." [7] This is similar in spirit to Rosenthal's work since it also deals with what might be called "propaganda" effects. The film in this case is "Tomorrow the World" an anti-Nazi commercial production. The experimental design, however, is less refined. There is no control group as an outside check on the results, and the movie was not introduced into the classroom as in the case of the Rosenthal experiment, so that the investigator could make sure that all his subjects were exposed to it.

But Wiese and Cole did collect background information on the school children who were studied, and they could trace the differences in effect among different sorts of children. They were enabled by this means to discover that the socio-economic position of the respondent played a considerable part in the

[7] Wiese, M. J., and Cole, S. G., "A Study of Children's Attitudes and the Influence of a Commercial Motion Picture," *Journal of Psychology*, 1946, No. 21.

sort of effect a movie might have. The poorer Negro children, for instance, were less likely than the others to see the value of kindness and education in correcting the Nazi tendencies of young people, and were more likely to think that nothing could be done about the situation. An important social datum was thus collected that tended to define much more closely the nature of the effect.

LEARNING THROUGH MOTION PICTURES

It has been estimated that in 1947 some fifty thousand motion picture projectors were in use in schools in the United States.[8] There has been a correspondingly high interest among educators in the effectiveness of film presentation of educational material. For this reason, and because the classroom provides good opportunities for experimentation, a considerable number of effect studies have been conducted on the information derived and retained from educational films.

These studies have all had one of two main purposes. Some of them, the earlier studies particularly, have been concerned with the effectiveness of film presentation as opposed to the conventional, oral method of teaching, and almost without exception they have indicated that more knowledge is gained and remembered by the film method. When tests are given after the experiment, the film-taught group makes better marks than the orally taught group.

Other studies are concerned more with the various methods by which film material may be presented. Does a discussion prove to be more effective when it is conducted after the film or when it is conducted before? Or to quote from one study, will a film shown twice, with a discussion between, prove substantially more effective than merely a single showing followed by a discussion? As far as methods go, the same problems are encountered with each sort of study, so we shall treat them simultaneously.

All the studies reported here are controlled experiments,

---

[8] See Floyd E. Brooker, "Motion Pictures as an Aid to Education," *Annals of the American Academy of Political and Social Science,* November, 1947.

either of the "comparative" type—in which those exposed to the stimulus (film) are compared with those who are not, or of the "simultaneous" type, in which *different* stimuli are introduced and the results compared. They differ in this fashion but, more significantly, they differ in the fashion in which the "control" is brought about. The problem is, of course, to match the groups so that the differences found in later tests can be taken as the result of the film presentation, rather than as the result of some other characteristic—such as an initial difference in intelligence between the two groups.

Most of the studies have attempted to solve the problem by selecting classes of students which are *on the average* similar in respect to background or mental characteristics. In a work by Arnspiger,[9] for instance, involving some 2,500 students in five different cities, the classes who saw films were matched in respect to social background with those who were instructed by the usual methods. In another large-scale study conducted by a group at the University of Chicago,[10] the classes were matched in respect to age and also in respect to mental age, as measured by standard tests and achievement in school. In a third study conducted among New Haven school children, mental age and the teacher's judgment as to ability were the main criteria for the matching,[11] and in yet another study, the groups were equated according to socio-economic status and intelligence quotient.[12] Whatever the particular criteria, the purpose was to eliminate extraneous influences.

One difficulty in equating groups according to *average* similarity in respect to a characteristic such as mental age or intelligence quotient, or marks on some previous examination, is that account may not be taken of the *distribution* within the

[9] Arnspiger, V. C., *Measuring the Effectiveness of Sound Pictures as Teaching Aids* (Teachers College, Columbia University, 1933).

[10] Freeman, F. N. (ed), *Visual Education: A Comparative Study of Motion Pictures and Other Methods of Instruction* (Chicago: University of Chicago Press, 1924).

[11] Knowlton, D. C., and Tilton, J. W., *Motion Pictures in History Teaching* (New Haven: Yale University Press, 1929).

[12] Eichel, C. G., "An Experiment to Determine the Most Effective Method of Teaching Current History," *Journal of Experimental Education*, 1940, No. 9.

group of the factors. The same over-all average on a test, for instance, might be obtained by a class of students, half of whom did very well and half of whom did very poorly, as is obtained from a class in which all the students received middling grades; but the reaction of the two groups to subsequent material could be quite different.

This difficulty has been overcome in some studies by a method involving the matching of students rather than of classes. Hanser, in his study of retention of knowledge among high school students,[13] formed two groups, each member of which was matched with a member of the other group according to mental age, intelligence quotient, and amount of factual knowledge on the subject of the film. He thus made sure that the distribution of these three elements was identical in his control and experimental groups.

In a few works on educational films, the problem of comparable control groups has been circumvented by means of rotational experiments, in which control and experimental groups are switched in subsequent presentations of films. A study by J. J. Weber among seventh grade students might be taken to illustrate this method.[14] Weber wished to test the effectiveness of this different method of presenting the same material by the "conventional" technique of an oral lesson followed by a review, by a film preceded by a lesson, and by a film followed by a lesson.

Three classes were chosen which happened to be not too closely equated in significant characteristics. Then, for the first unit of the experiment, class A was given the lesson and review, class B shown a film and then given oral instruction, and for class C the lesson preceded the film. In the subsequent two units of the experiment, new films were chosen of the same length and type but differing in subject matter; and the three methods

[13] Hanser, J. E., "The Effect of Educational Motion Pictures upon the Retention of Informational Learning," *Journal of Experimental Education*, 1933, No. 2.

[14] Weber, J. J., *Comparative Effectiveness of Some Visual Aids in Seventh Grade Instruction* (Chicago: Educational Screen, Inc., 1922).

of presentation were interchanged. Schematically, the entire experiment appears as follows:

	Film I "Indian Scenes"	Film II "Chinese Scenes"	Film III "Japanese Scenes"
Group A	lesson-review	film-lesson	lesson-film
Group B	film-lesson	lesson-film	lesson-review
Group C	lesson-film	lesson-review	film-lesson

Each group, therefore, was exposed to each type of presentation.

After each of the three units, a test was given by the investigator to see how much factual knowledge had been gained through the various methods. The scores for each type of presentation were then averaged and the total average scores obtained were as follows:

Film-Lesson	Lesson-Film	Lesson-Review
52.43	50.63	46.93

These differences found between film and oral presentation cannot be attributed to differences between the groups tested, since each group was subjected to each method, and only the *combined* scores were used.

The over-all findings of these studies on educational films, as has been suggested above, is that film presentation is more effective in the gaining and retaining of knowledge than the older teaching techniques. We cannot, however, accept these findings as conclusive, until we have better evidence on the extent to which the *fact of being experimented upon* influenced the post-experiment performance of the groups exposed to films. It is quite possible that the novelty of the situation, and the fact of being singled out for special treatment, may have acted as special temporary stimuli to greater attention to the presentation and greater efforts on any subsequent tests. A lesson might be taken here from a comparable situation in certain industrial studies conducted to determine factors influencing workers' output. In one study, practically every change that was introduced to selected groups of workers resulted in increased output

—regardless of the nature of the change. The workers were apparently responding to the experimental situation rather than to the stimulus.[15]

The implications of this for visual aids to education is obvious; if it is only the experimental situation that is causing the apparent increase in learning, then we could expect a return to normal after film-education becomes established as the usual method of teaching for any group of students. So far, to the author's knowledge, no studies have been conducted over an extended period for the purpose of discovering whether the greater effectiveness of visual over oral education gradually wears away.

There are other areas as well, in respect to education through motion pictures, that remain largely unexplored. Most of the studies limit themselves, understandably, to a measurement of what students have learned and retained of a factual nature. This is, of course, the sort of "effect" of films that is most amenable to objective measurement, but we are left with very little knowledge of how effective films may be, for instance, in instilling manual ability, or, to give a quite dissimilar example, to develop abilities of conceptualization. An interesting exception to the general rule is a very early study (1919) by J. V. Lacy [16] in which it was discovered that in this particular instance, hearing a story told gave the students a better ability to "draw inferences" and to "make moral discriminations" than either the method of reading the same material or of seeing it presented as a motion picture.

Another insufficiently explored area is that of the relationship between the characteristics of the audiences and the nature and extent of the effect which films have. It may very well be that there are certain social types or psychological types of individuals much better able than others to learn certain things through films. We have already discussed a study by May and Shuttleworth on the differences between moviegoers and non-

15 See Roethlisberger, F. J., and Dickson, W. J., *Management and the Worker* (Cambridge: Harvard University Press, 1938).

16 Lacy, J. V., *The Relative Value of Motion Pictures as an Educational Agency*. Teachers College, Columbia University, November, 1919.

moviegoers. A corollary study might be undertaken to discover what differences exist between those who do and those who do not learn from movies.

The Research Branch of the War Department conducted a series of investigations to determine the effect on learning of a combined film strip presentation and audience participation.[17] The results of the studies are of great significance and are therefore presented later in this chapter.

The importance of participation by students has been emphasized by numerous studies which have found that recall of verbal material is greatly facilitated if the time spent in studying is divided between reading the material and attempting to recall it. The purpose of the War Department experiment was to determine whether the principle of participation can be utilized in film instructions.

The educational objective of the test studies was the learning of the phonetic alphabet which is used by Signal Corps men in the Army (Able for A, Baker for B, etc.) A "standard" and an "experimental" film strip was used to permit the comparative analyses. In both film strips the phonetic names corresponding to each letter in the alphabet were shown on the screen and pronounced by the narrator. Each phonetic name was accompanied also by a picture designed to create an association between the letter and the name. Partial and complete review lists were shown interspersed at regular intervals, and at the end of the alphabet.

The difference between the "experimental" and "standard" film strip was that in the latter all review lists presented each phonetic name with its corresponding letter while they were enunciated by the narrator; in the "experimental" strip, however, the letters in the review lists were followed by question marks and the names were to be called off by the participants.

The results showed that the active recitation method increased considerably the degree of recollection as compared with the standard presentation. The effect of participation was

[17] Hovland, C. I., Lumsdaine, A. A., and Sheffield, F. D., *Experiments on Mass Communications*, p. 228.

found to be greater for the more difficult phonetic names than for the easier names. The tests also demonstrated that men with lower levels of mental ability profited more from the audience participation procedure than those with higher mental test scores. Less improvement was noted when motivation was increased by announcing that the men would be tested on the

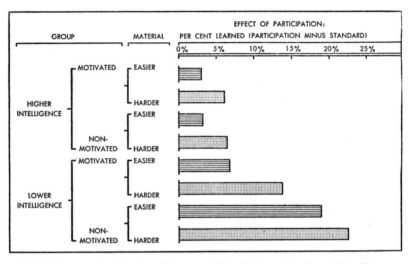

CHART 8. Contribution of audience participation as a function of intelligence, motivation, and difficulty of material. (From *Experiments on Mass Communications.*)

instructions covered, and better recollection was also found due to participation when men were not given a special motivation to learn. Audience participation becomes, therefore, most effective when intelligence and motivation are lower and when the difficulty of learning is greater. Chart 8 shows the gains in learning due to participation, taking into account intelligence levels, motivation, and material of varying difficulty. The experiment was conducted at a reception center, using 742 enlisted men.

Three factors are considered to be mainly responsible for the improvement produced by participation. First, active participation insures the rehearsal of responses which are to be learned. Another advantage is that this procedure provides, in effect, a series of examinations covering the various segments of the presentation. This motivational factor may be particularly effective since the participants would realize that their immediate neighbors would note how much they had absorbed of the subject matter. The desire to make a good impression during active recitation would motivate many respondents to pay more attention during the time of the presentation when they take only a passive part. A third factor which seems to indicate the advisability of the participation method is that practice is required under stimulus conditions similar to those in which the participants will later be expected to perform the responses to be learned.

REACTIONS TO MOTION PICTURES

An entirely different sort of effect of movies is the immediate response of people to its content. The reaction or response to a movie does not necessarily indicate any particular long-range effect. Disgust or disapproval of a scene may be the result of a resistance that will mitigate any future effect. And a person's favorable response may or may not indicate what he learns from a movie, or how he will otherwise be affected by it. Studies of audience reaction are therefore just a first step in studies of effect on behavior, or learning, or attitude changes.

It might be illuminating to record here a study that was done on an educational film to obtain the reaction of a typical adult audience in such a form that methods of making better educational films might be suggested. The study, under the general direction of Adolf Sturmthal, was made possible by a grant from the Alfred P. Sloan Foundation.[18] The experiments were conducted by J. N. Peterman and the analysis upon which this account is based was done by A. Curtis. The films were tested by means of the Lazarsfeld-Stanton program analyzer, a device described in Chapter 4.

Among the films submitted to this testing procedure was "Valley Town," produced by the Educational Film Institute of

[18] See Sturmthal, A., and Curtis, A., "Program Analyzer Tests of Two Educational Films," *Radio Research, 1942–43.*

New York University. Thirteen groups, totaling 190 respondents, were used, the groups consisting of college and high school students, members of businessmen's associations, unions, participants in YMCA and YWCA gatherings, church groups, and housewives.

The investigators found the program analyzer a surprisingly sensitive instrument for registering audience response and for eliciting the recall of part-by-part responses in interviewing. For this purpose the script was broken down into sequences, and the reactions studied. The reactions were examined separately for various groups among the subjects, and group breakdowns by sex and education were made. Program analyzer reactions were also studied separately for persons who had experienced unemployment for at least three months, and those who had not had such an experience. The very interesting group differences can be touched upon only very briefly.

"Valley Town" is concerned with the problem of technological unemployment. It shows a community in two different periods—in prosperity, and then in depression aggravated by technological unemployment; and it brings in a single family as an illustration of the later condition.

An average of 27 per cent of the subjects registered "liking" per time-unit of the film; and an average of 10.3 per cent registered "disliking." It should be kept in mind, however, that it is not the average figures which matter. They are useful mainly in spotting the major deviations in reactions. A detailed film-profile, showing the reactions per three-second intervals, was obtained.

To facilitate the analysis of reactions, the script of "Valley Town" can be divided into fifteen sequences. It is mainly the extremes, that is, the peaks of the "like" and "dislike" reactions, which are described here. The percentages given show the proportion of people who registered "like" or "dislike" for a given section of the film.

The following material is reprinted from *Radio Research, 1942–43.*

Sequence no.	Time	Subjects' reactions on the program analyzer
1. Titles and credits	0–1:15	Both likes and dislikes remain few, with some increase of likes during a printed commentary: "The people are not actors," etc.
2. Day begins in V. T. Impersonal symbols of rooftops through early morning haze and smoke. The commentator-mayor describes the town where men and women lived by machines and bought machine-made goods.	1:15–2:07	The liking stays below average throughout this sequence, rising to about 20 per cent at the first pan shot of rooftops and the mayor's introductory remarks, with dislikes decreasing to 11 per cent for this same shot.[3]
3. Day begins for the people—more personalized. People begin to go to their work. A train pulls up at the station. People breakfast in a lunchroom. Two men walk to work together.	2:07–3:30	Liking increases to about average at first shot of a person—a long angle shot of man walking at 2:09; up to 31 per cent at 2:48—first shot of a locomotive backing at station. Dislikes stay below average.
4. More machines, more jobs; men arrive at the factory. Men work at a power press. Several shots of a lathe in operation, a few shots of a power loom. The	3:30–5:36	The several lathe shots much liked, those of *man behind lathe with calipers the fifth most-liked shot,* by 40 per cent. Liking declines as lathe shots go on,

[3] Likes and dislikes can of course increase simultaneously, coming from different respondents.

Sequence no.	Time	Subjects' reactions on the program analyzer
commentary stresses the untroubled times when men were easily adapted to the new machines.		and for power loom. Dislikes at a minimum through this.
5. Steel mill, old style; steel rolling process which used many skillful men meant still more jobs in Valley Town.	5:36–8:06	*Fourth most-liked shot in film—41 per cent at 6:18–24 of man putting steel sheet under roller.* 39 per cent at 6:42–54, more shots of steel shifted on roller. Liking declines as this goes on. *Fifth most-disliked shot, disliked by 17 per cent, occurs at 7:42–45, man at rollers with light from behind.*
6. Good times for the people in Valley Town: a street scene at Christmas time, filled with shoppers. The mayor says, "We thought prosperity would last forever."	8:06–9:03	Seen with indifference, both likes and dislikes below average. A close-up of young couple's faces at store window fairly well liked by 30 per cent.
7. A train symbolizes the exchange of goods between Valley Town and the rest of the world. A quick succession of shots of a locomotive and a whole train. Commentary: "And then the wheels stopped."	9:03–10:24	*Second most-liked shot in the film is the locomotive at 6:11, again at 6:24—44 per cent. Liking goes down, dislike mounts at 10:06 for train wheels whizzing past and receding.*

Sequence no.	Time	Subjects' reactions on the program analyzer
8. The deserted streets and factories of Valley Town when the wheels stop. "It wasn't the fault of the machines . . . in fact machines do often create jobs but now there was a depression. . . ."	10:24–11:36	Likes mostly about average in this sequence, the highest 34 per cent at 10:48 of man pushing wheelbarrow down deserted street. Dislikes a little above average, most so for same shot at 10:48, and 11:21, inactive steel rollers.
9. Automatic steel milling process, white hot ingots, handled by one man at the controls.	11:36–12:45	Increase in liking to 39 per cent for steel ingot under spray at 12:24, then liking declines through rest of sequence. Dislikes average to below average here.
10. An unemployed man walks home through an alley where he sees his neighbors in poverty and idleness. He thinks about their dilemma and wonders, "What am I going home for?"	12:45–14:51	Liking stays at about 30 per cent, but dislikes about double the average—20 per cent, especially for two men cutting rubber patch, dog at garbage pail, woman throwing out trash.
11. The unemployed man's wife prepares a meager dinner and serves it. A mournful song describes her thoughts and fears.	14:51–19:03	Likes and dislikes about average till *song begins,* then liking drops and *dislikes go to highest point,* over 30 per cent. More normal when song ends.
12. The mill smokestacks	19:03–20:12	Likes work up through

Sequence no.	*Time*	*Subjects' reactions on the program analyzer*
are cut down; a group of unemployed men watching as the smokestacks fall.		shots of torch-operator cutting smokestacks and men watching operation to *third highest liking of 43 per cent at 19:42—close-ups of two men watching.* Liking declines but stays above average as stacks fall. Dislikes low throughout.
13. The men leave the scene and crouch around a bonfire in the ruins of a building, to mull over their problem. The commentator talks of their need for learning new skills, the need for retraining and what it has cost the country in the man-years-of-work-experience lost.	20:12–23:27	Likes below average for this part and dislikes above average, especially between 21:39 and 22:39 as men sit around talking in own voices.
14. Help wanted once more. The war emergency creates jobs.	23:27–23:50	Drop in liking for want ad, then a rise to 30 per cent as retraining plea goes on. Dislikes few.
15. Retraining for new jobs and new skills. Men at work again on machines. Shots of men at work on machines and airplanes are accompanied by	23:50–25:03 end	Increase in liking fairly regularly to *highest point in film for very last shot—close-up of man with hair blowing in propeller wash.*

Sequence no.	*Time*	*Subjects' reactions on the program analyzer*
an exhortation to keep our workers up to date—to remember the lesson we have learned.		

The reasons given during the interviewing period aided greatly in the interpretation of the program analyzer reactions. The most frequent "like" comments referred to the action or process shown in the film. Such references were made particularly for the machine sequence 4 and the train sequence 7. The subjects enjoyed these sequences either because they "liked machines" or because they found their rhythmic motion esthetically or emotionally appealing.

I liked the machines, the rhythm and the movement. I just enjoyed watching it. Especially later on, the rhythm as a whole and in the man's footwork.

The excellent photography was a second major reason for enjoyment. It was mentioned particularly for the train sequence 7, also for sequences 5 (old steel mill) and 12 (cutting down of smokestacks). If the train sequence 7 was criticized, it was mainly for its length, the subjects explaining that "too many machines turning" became monotonous.

Sequence 8, which showed the stopped wheels and the deserted streets, was liked for the contrast to the preceding sequences of motion.

I liked the contrast between the tempo of the train, first going so fast, then faster, then the sudden stopping. It was dramatic, you realized something drastic had happened.

Similar comments on the contract, and also references to an expected action, were made for sequence 10, the unemployed man walking home through streets with poverty stricken, idle neighbors, and for sequence 11, showing him in his own depressing home.

I liked his walk home, because a sort of plot was coming up. It was beginning to get you wondering what was going to happen.

On the other hand, for both these scenes with the unemployed man, dislike reactions increased. The comments show the reason. Many of the subjects did not care for the deprivational character implied in these scenes. "It showed that there was nothing left to do. Left a feeling of despair." Comments of this type were the most frequent criticisms.

Conversely, the machine sequence 4 and the train sequence 7, both showing the activity preceding the depression, and sequence 14, showing the availability of jobs created through the war emergency, were liked for their indulgent character.[19]

I remember definitely when this started I was still enjoying the pictures of the machinery, and then I think I changed when they showed the working conditions that weren't too good, and then they led you back to the feeling of prosperity. I liked it then. The people were getting by and the young people were getting jobs in stores and so on. It was definitely good.

Comments referring to the music were rather contradictory. It was liked in sequence 7, where it underlined the activity of the trains, the machines, and the town.

I liked the music. It fitted in with the wheels turning.

The music was disliked, however, in sequence 11, where the unemployed man's wife was singing a mournful song describing her fears and thoughts.

I don't think it was appropriate to have the girl sing that part. It would have been more impressive if she had spoken in a simple manner.

This song was the most disliked part of the whole production. The charting of reactions according to personal characteristics of the subjects tested gave some interesting results.

[19] The terms "indulgence" and "deprivation" are derived from an unpublished classification system for content symbols in films, by Harold Lasswell and Dorothy Jones. "Indulgent" qualifies those scenes which convey pleasant, hopeful, optimistic feelings and ideas; "deprivation" those which express hopelessness, loss of status or ability to function.

The film was liked consistently more by males, particularly the sequence of the lathe, those of the old and the new steel-rolling processes, the destruction of the mill smokestacks, and the last, retraining sequence. Males also showed more numerous dislike reactions, particularly for the woman's song. Some exceptional parts more disliked by females were the more "disgusting" shots of poverty on the unemployed man's walk home, the depression street scene, the lathe and power loom. The males' likes predominate over the females' more than their dislikes. Women are more indifferent throughout, fewer of them registering either likes or dislikes.

Differences by education are less clear-cut than those by sex. In general, the chart for the less-educated indicates more frequent liking by them, and the line of the higher-educated shows more frequent dislikes. Exceptional parts more liked by the higher-educated are the lathe shots, the first part of the old style steel-rolling mill, the automatic strip processes, and most markedly the help wanted and retraining sequence. The higher-educated dislike more strongly the unemployed family sequence, particularly the song, the walk home of the unemployed man, the first part of the sequence showing the men leaving the scene of the cut-down smokestacks. This would indicate a particular liking of the higher-educated for the gaining, "indulgent" aspects of the film and particular dislike of the deprivational. Does this come from greater conservatism, or greater previous realization that these facts and conditions exist and therefore greater impatience with having them driven home in this way?

Persons who have been unemployed like the film more on the whole than others. But they do not begin to express stronger liking until after the first four sequences, or six minutes. At the beginning of each new sequence they drop in their liking below the others, and recover their majority liking only after some delay, varying in length with the material shown. It looks as though they are more wary about committing themselves to positive responses before they know what the slant of the picture is, as a whole, and of each new sequence. When they know, they go ahead of the others in their degree of approval. Their liking stands above that of others most clearly in those sequences which show the effect of unemployment upon people.

One of the Payne Fund studies, *The Emotional Responses of Children to the Motion Picture Situation*,[20] deals with the question of reaction through the use of another sort of mechanical device, a psychogalvanometer, measuring body changes. The subjects under investigation, adults and children of various ages, were exposed to motion pictures selected for their portrayal of scenes of "danger" and "sex."

The greatest reaction to danger scenes was found in the six- to twelve-year-old group, the greatest reaction to love scenes among younger children. Such a physiological study is useful in comparing differences among various kinds of children. In this case, sex differences were found to be negligible, but individual variations were very marked.

In general studies of this kind would be more useful if there were further analysis of the individual variations which were noted. What kind of children react most violently and how do their reactions affect their subsequent development?

The most thoroughgoing work in the field of response to motion pictures has been done by Karl Buhler and Katherine Wolf at the Psychological Institute of the University of Vienna. They conducted some thirty-one studies of motion pictures in the period 1932–38, all of which, unfortunately, remain unpublished.

Some of these studies fall under the heading of content analysis. They analyzed, for example, expressive movements in motion pictures; they compared presentations of similar material in books, in motion pictures, and on the legitimate stage. Other studies were concerned with the portrayal of time and space in motion pictures, the use of symbols, of humor, the role of language, and the formal structure of the movies. Most of these content analyses, however, were accompanied by reaction studies which determined, for example, when the portrayal of

[20] Dysinger, W. S., and Ruckmick, Christian A., *The Emotional Responses of Children to the Motion Picture Situation* (New York: Macmillan, 1933).

time or space is understood and when it is not understood, what is considered funny and by whom, and how many expressive movements an actor can make without appearing grotesque on the one hand or stilted on the other.

The rest of the studies were concerned largely with the nature of the moviegoing experience. Thus, they studied the role of identification, the after-effects of seeing films of various kinds, changes in star preferences over a period of time, and so on. Lacking details as to techniques and results, the chief value of this work for motion picture research in this country is that it suggests the richness of a largely unexplored field, which would not only throw light on our understanding of what movies do to people, but would also help us to understand people by analyzing their reactions to various motion picture situations.

The whole question of response to motion pictures and the reasons for people's responding in the way they do needs a great deal more investigation. It is clear from the little evidence already gathered that some such process as identification is involved in the moviegoing experience. This phenomenon was also discussed in chapter 9, section "The Drawing Power of Male and Female Stars for Moviegoers of Their Own Sex," but for the most part the nature of the process is still unknown. How close to the viewer's own situation must the situation portrayed in the movie be, for instance? Under what sort of social pressures do people become most susceptible to the process? Some of the work that has already been done on the needs and gratifications of audiences of specific radio programs offers leads that might well be followed up in the movie field.

Herzog, for instance, through depth interviews has been able to discover some of the motivations of people listening to quiz programs and to daytime serials.[21]

EFFECT STUDIES BY THE WAR DEPARTMENT

During World War II, a series of research studies were made by the War Department to measure the effectiveness of special

[21] See Herzog, Herta, "What Do We Really Know about Daytime Serial Listeners?" *Radio Research, 1942–43.*

Army films for servicemen. The studies were made by the Experimental Section of the Research Branch in the Information and Education Division. After the war the findings accumulated by this body were released to a civilian committee of the Social Science Research Council, which is supported by the Carnegie Foundation. A special committee of the Council evaluated the data and prepared a four-volume series, *Studies in Social Psychology in World War II*. The third volume [22] deals mainly with research studies covering motion pictures. The films discussed include the first four of the "Why We Fight" series produced for the Information and Education Division to explain the background of World War II.

The studies of the War Department dealt mainly with orientation (indoctrination) and training films. They aimed to determine whether, and to what extent, the films succeeded in imparting information to the men, in changing their opinions in the desired direction and, in the last analysis, increasing their motivation to fight. The ultimate goal of using overt behavioral changes as criteria of effectiveness could not be attained in the testing of most of the films. It was, however, possible to trace actual changes the films produced in the orientation of their audiences. Checks of this type are usually not possible for commercial pictures [23] and they proved to be a valuable contribution to communications research.

The Research Branch used frequently the following two different experimental designs in the evaluative studies of the pictures. One method termed as the "after-only" design called for a test at a time after the film was shown to determine the factual knowledge and opinion in a "film group" which saw the film and a "control group" which did not see the film. The second method termed "before-after" design involved the measuring of factual knowledge and opinion both before and after exposure to the medium. The "after-only" design is considered superior from the standpoint of being easier to ad-

[22] *Experiments on Mass Communications.*

[23] An exception is Dore Schary's "Crossfire"; controlled studies revealed that the picture resulted in a decrease of race prejudice among persons who had seen it

minister and less subject to the possibility that the measuring process will bias the results obtained. The "before-after" method permits a better basis for analysis and better sampling. Due to the apparent comparability of the results obtained with the two procedures the "after-only" design was considered adequate in many studies.

The effect studies on indoctrination films were conducted usually one week after the screening. The assumption that effects would be maximal immediately after the screening was justified in case of factual information. Many opinion items, however, showed increments rather than decrements with the lapse of time.[24]

The Research Branch made a valuable contribution to communications effect research through the development of an effect measure termed the effectiveness index. As a rule the effect of a medium is measured by comparing the proportion of a key response in a control group with the proportion of the key response in the experimental group. The following figures taken from a study conducted for "The Battle of Britain" show that the film in the respective area of orientation resulted in a 15 per cent change of the men's interpretation.[25] The sample under analysis totaled twelve hundred persons.

Question: The heavy bombing attacks on Britain were part of an attempt by the Nazis to . . . CHECK ONE (of four possible answers).

	Percentage of men checking the key answer: "Invade and Conquer England"
Control Group	43%
Film Group	58

The "key answer" is the critical one, the response of which the film was calculated to change. It is the one used in the measurement of the film's effectiveness both in changing opinions and factual information. A straight percentage difference as demonstrated above between film and control groups was considered to have certain limitations in determining the impact of the medium, especially when different effects are com-

---

[24] *Experiments on Mass Communications*, p. 182.
[25] *Ibid.*, p. 34.

pared. The measure of effect is a function of the prevalent level of frequency of the key response prior to the experiment. Consequently, if most members of a population are not informed about a particular fact prior to the film exposure, the film can show a large change when effects are measured in this way. But if most members of the population are already familiar with the fact prior to the film exposure, the film will show only a small effect. Different initial knowledge of a certain fact may stem from socio-economic, educational, and age differences of various populations.

The "effectiveness index" neutralizes the bias inherent in straight percentage differences by measuring the increase in the number checking the correct response divided by the *maximum increase possible* as a baseline.[26]

If P_1 is used to indicate the initial per cent and P_2 the final per cent, the effectiveness index is expressed by the following formula:

$$\text{Effectiveness Index} = 100 \times \frac{P_2 - P_1}{100 - P_1}$$

The following illustration [27] taken from the study of "The Battle of Britain" shows effects measured in three different ways. The example shows how the conclusion is altered by using less appropriate measures which are biased by ceiling effects.

	Per Cent Answering Correctly	
	Reason British Navy could not be used	British military equipment after fall of France
Control group	36%	5%
Film group	55	18
Effect measured as difference between per cents	19	13
Effect measured as per cent improvement	53	260
Effect measured from base of maximum increase possible (effectiveness index)	30	14

Substituting the values of the example pertaining to "Reason British Navy could not be used" the effectiveness index is computed as follows:

[26] *Ibid.,* p. 285.
[27] *Ibid.,* p. 287.

$$\text{E.I.} = 100\text{x}\,\frac{55 - 36}{100 - 36} = 29.7$$

The effectiveness index is not designed to take into account psychological factors such as the likelihood that when the initial acceptance of an opinion is high, the few individuals who differ in their opinion would be especially resistant to change, or the likelihood that an extremely unpopular opinion also reflects special resistance to change. An opinion held by, say, only 10 per cent of the population may often be one the population is predisposed against believing and resistant to change.

Evaluative research such as that conducted for "The Battle of Britain" may show different effects on different levels of the investigation. This film, for example, had marked effects on the men's knowledge of the factual material leading up to the war. The film had also some marked effects on opinion test items, where they specifically covered the factors involved in a particular interpretation. Such opinion changes were, however, less frequent and less marked than the changes of factual knowledge. The film had very few effects on opinion items of more general nature which were considered the criteria for determining the effectiveness of the films in achieving their orientation objectives. The film had no effects on the men's motivation to serve as soldiers, which was considered the ultimate objective of the orientation program.

The lack of effects of the films upon general opinions gave room for various hypothetical explanations. The amount of men's motivations which could be effected by a fifty-minute film was very insignificant in relation to the other motivational factors present in their total life situation. The studies covered only single films. One study, however, in which the cumulative effects of two pictures were analyzed, did not show a sizable increase of effects on general opinions or motivations. Also, it may be that the area of influence might have been saturated by civilian sources before entry into the service. Finally, it may be assumed that such a program may influence only a small part of the population whose attitudes are primarily determined by rationalizations, as compared to the larger segment of the population which acquires motivations and attitudes generally through nonrational channels.

The War Department studies determined also the relation between the audience's evaluation of the film and its effects on their opinions on factual knowledge. Men who liked the film most tended to be most influenced by it. But it is difficult to rule out the possibility that those who liked the film were different initially in other respects from those who did not like it. It was also determined that men who regarded the film as propagandistic were somewhat less affected; but also in this case the causal relationship is difficult to establish from the results.

A study designed to measure the effect of a certain communication on an audience may serve to examine also the time element in relation to the impact of the message. The War Department's Research Branch studied this problem in line with the investigations carried out for the film "The Battle of Britain." [28] The results of this study were in part quite unexpected, and invite further experimentations in this field to determine whether generalizations of the findings are permissible.

The analysis of the tests showed the necessity of differentiating between "factual knowledge" items (example: *Luftwaffe* is the name of the German Air Force) and "opinion" items (example: The British are doing their fair share in the fighting). The degree of retention of factual material by the men tested after a lapse of time fell into a pattern anticipated by the experimenters. The mean score of ten fact-quiz items, obtained nine weeks after the exposure to the film, was slightly less than half as great as that obtained in the short-time measurement, i.e., about one week after the screening. In contrast to that the results for "opinion" items did not show an over-all decrease after the interval of nine weeks. Instead, while some items showed the anticipated decrement, others showed a reliable increase after the nine-week period, resulting in a mean effect slightly greater for the long-time measurement than for the short time tabulation. An analysis of these unexpected results indicated that increases of opinion changes, with the passage of time, more

[28] *Ibid.*, p. 182.

likely occur in the case of "uninformed opinions," especially among persons of lower educational levels.

Various hypotheses were offered to explain this interesting phenomenon. It was suggested, for example, that increments in opinion changes with the lapse of time are in part a function of predisposition for belief in a certain direction, and that this projective factor is more likely to show up in the case of general statements than in the case of highly specific statements. In addition it may be possible that specific material tends to become more general with the lapse of time. The existence of a projective factor, and a shift from specific to general, would work in combination to produce increments in the more "attitudinal" items, and in the direction toward which the individual was already predisposed.[29]

As shown before, the film "The Battle of Britain" left marked effect on the men's factual knowledge, and lesser effects were noted with regard to the change-of-opinion items. If we enter the time element into the analysis we find that factual items with the highest immediate effect show a considerable decrement with the lapse of time. Some opinion items, on the other hand, were not affected by the passage of time and show in some cases reliable increment. Research studies in other fields demonstrate that people do not like "being influenced." It may be speculated therefore that some members of the soldier audience who felt the impact of the orientation films after the showing may have been unwilling to concede a change in opinion at that time. A lapse of nine weeks, however, may have in some cases cemented the change in opinion which then became evident in long-time measurements. Time analyses in effect studies may gain more prominence in future studies of this kind.

[29] *Ibid.*, p. 275.

CHAPTER 13 *The theater and*

admission prices

At the beginning of 1950 there were almost twenty thousand conventional theaters operating in the United States, with a combined capacity of close to twelve million seats. A study conducted by the Motion Picture Association of America in 1948 showed an average seating capacity of 643 seats per theater. After World War II a new type of exhibition in the form of drive-in theaters came into existence. First considered a sort of freak exhibition, drive-ins mushroomed all over the country and reached an estimated fifteen hundred units at the beginning of 1950.

The place of exhibition itself may be the object of intense research studies. The purpose of analytical surveys conducted for the theater management may be to determine the composition of the particular audiences. Studies are also done to ascertain how the patrons feel about the physical aspects of the theater, especially to determine whether the customers find fault with any phase of the theater's operation—such as the cleanliness of the auditorium and washrooms, the quality of the seats, the air conditioning. The likes and dislikes of the programs offered can be investigated, to find out how they compare with competing houses, and with those theaters which show the same pictures before or after they are presented in the theater under observation. Interest in added attractions such as bingo or stage shows may also be determined. Areas from which a house draws the bulk of its audience may be charted, and competition areas where the audiences of two or more houses overlap can be defined.

Theater studies are, in many instances, requested by the head office of a theater chain. This is done not only to check on the efficiency of the management of different theaters, but to show theater officials how their own place looks to an unbiased paying customer. A manager who sees his theater for many hours every day cannot help overlooking some shortcomings which may register immediately with the patron.

As a rule, theater surveys are conducted for neighborhood houses. The issues involved may vary from case to case and there are no general rules as to the approach which should be used. Some of the basic techniques used by the Motion Picture Research Bureau for most surveys of this type may be of interest.

The fieldwork is usually carried out within easy walking distance, or within the radius of approximately half a mile of the theater. House-to-house canvassing is done for these assignments to make sure of contacting persons who actually live near the theater.

Whenever feasible the area in which the poll is going to take place is divided into a "competition area" and a "non-competition area." Interviews conducted in the former usually yield information as to how the theater under investigation is affected by the other theaters in the neighborhood. Interviews recorded in the latter, usually the more important area, show more detailed information about the theater itself. Here we find negative comments made by respondents who for some reason or another prefer to walk a little farther to see a picture less conveniently located for them than the theater for which the test is made.

The patrons, actual and potential, of a neighborhood theater may be divided into three different categories. Moviegoers who attend the theater regularly or quite frequently, moviegoers who seldom visit the theater, and moviegoers who do not patronize it at all.

It has proved advantageous to divide the sample into these three groups and to phrase questions differently for each one of the three categories. Thus, patrons who attend quite often are asked: "Is there anything about this theater you especially like or dislike?" And respondents who state that they seldom visit the theater are asked: "Why don't you go to this theater more frequently?" Those who stated in the categorizing question that they never patronize the theater—usually the most important respondents for this kind of research study—are asked: "Why don't you ever go to this theater?"

This set of key questions usually registers any defects of theater maintenance or of program arrangement which did not comply with the wishes of the patrons.

Sometimes a theater which is in perfect shape may have a bad reputation, either entirely erroneously or based on a past condition. In one actual case a theater was considered dirty by a large proportion of its patrons even though a new management had taken great pains to correct the condition. A survey which revealed these circumstances prompted the management to launch an advertising campaign, pointing out to its potential customers that the house had been taken over by a new owner who did his best to keep it clean. An increase in attendance showed that the campaign had the desired result.

The new drive-in theaters have created some questions in the minds of distributors and theater operators who have been confronted with conflicting statements concerning the audiences of this new form of exhibition. Drive-in theater operators claim they are catering to an entirely new patronage, while other observers feel that the outdoor theaters are taking their audiences entirely from the rank and file of conventional moviegoers.

A number of research studies were conducted in various locations to obtain facts about the drive-in theater audience. Since these new theaters provide a rather novel form of entertainment, it may be some time until this new medium establishes its own attendance patterns and motivations. The studies conducted in this field show a number of features which may remain distinct characteristics of the drive-in theater audiences.

Drive-in theaters create new business. Many drive-in theater admissions are due solely to the unique qualities of this form of exhibition. A large portion of the drive-in theater audience is composed of regular moviegoers who would not have attended a conventional theater on the day of the drive-in theater attendance.

Attendance in one's own car affords certain privileges important to the moviegoer. There is the possibility of taking along small children, eliminating in that way the baby-sitter problem which makes heavy inroads on the box-office of conventional theaters. There is no need of dressing up and the drive-in patron can eat, drink, smoke, and talk undisturbed. Many people prefer the fresh air to the bad air or bad air-conditioning of some indoor theaters. Some persons cannot attend conventional theaters due to permanent or temporary disabilities.

Drive-ins are attended by large groups. The attendance unit of four persons is encountered most frequently, compared with the attendance unit of two persons prevailing in conventional theaters.

Surveys concerned with the operation of theaters often aim to determine the exposure to and effect of advertising originating with the theater under investigation, and of the competing houses. These are strictly advertising studies and outside the scope of this chapter.

A rather unique survey was conducted at the beginning of 1942 by the Motion Picture Research Bureau with the New York League for the Hard of Hearing. The use of hearing aids which are provided by some exhibitors in specially wired theaters was under observation.[1]

The survey was conducted by mail and was limited to the New York metropolitan area in which there are about 110,000 inhabitants afflicted with hearing defects, 10,000 of them children. At present about eighteen of the approximately seven hundred houses in New York City are equipped with special

[1] Handel, Leo, *Studies of the Motion Picture Audience*, p. 22.

hearing aids. Most of these theaters are concentrated in the Manhattan theater district.

Hard-of-hearing people, though not numerous enough to be of great commercial interest of themselves, influence to a large extent the movie habits of relatives and friends who attend with them.

The object of the study was to find out whether the attendance of hard-of-hearing people could be increased by equipping more theaters with hearing aids. The answers to the questions indicated that theaters with hearing aids would draw considerable patronage from this section of the audience.

The following comments were made repeatedly by respondents:

> There are not enough seats with hearing aids available.
> These seats should be reserved as long as others are available.
> These seats should be in a special favorably located section.
> These seats should be on the aisles.
> The hearing aids should be kept in perfect condition.
> Passes should be made available to get the hearing aids without paying a deposit.
> Theaters which have hearing aids should publicize it.

On the whole the survey pointed to the advisability of installing more and better distributed hearing aid devices.

In some isolated cases the theater management polls patrons to decide questions of policy connected with the operation of the theater. The Walter Reade circuit conducted a poll among patrons in Perth Amboy and Morristown, New Jersey, to determine whether or not Paramount's "Unconquered" and Warner's "Life with Father" should be shown in their theaters. Both pictures would have necessitated an increase of admission prices. Fifty-five per cent of the persons voting on the issue indicated they would pay the higher impost. The circuit did not program these pictures because it was felt that the result of the poll did not warrant booking of either of the pictures in those towns or in other communities where this circuit has theaters.[2]

[2] *Variety*, November 19, 1947.

MOTION PICTURE THEATER ADMISSION PRICE INDEXES

The trend of motion picture theater admission prices has been the subject of much discussion during the past few years. Claims and counterclaims have been made, inside and outside the industry, but definitive information on a nationwide scale is yet to be presented. For the most part, opinions have been based upon scattered evidence, superficial analysis, or hearsay.

In an attempt to obtain a more reliable indication of the true course of admission prices in recent years, the Motion Picture Association's Department of Research has requested, and has been given access to, unpublished price data collected by the Bureau of Labor Statistics, U. S. Department of Labor. Each month the Bureau computes a consumer's price index, formerly known as the cost of living index, which is a composite measure of prices charged for clothing, food, house furnishings, rent, fuel, electricity, and ice. In addition, selected miscellaneous commodities and services are covered, including admission prices charged by motion picture theaters.

The Bureau's index of admission prices for children and adults from March, 1941, through September, 1949, is shown in Table 66.

The Bureau's admission price index is based upon data collected from motion picture theaters in 34 selected cities in the United States. The index is determined from prices charged at evening performances, Monday through Friday, omitting admission scales for Saturday, Sunday, and holiday showings.

A local field representative of the Bureau in each of the thirty-four cities is responsible for securing the necessary data on prices. If the theater is readily accessible, the representative obtains the information by a personal call at the theater.

Not every motion picture house in each of the thirty-four cities is covered monthly by the Bureau representative. Instead, prices are sampled in selected downtown and neighborhood houses. Data for theaters with stage shows and vaudeville are not included in the index, as this factor is confined exclusively to theaters exhibiting motion pictures.

TABLE 66

MOTION PICTURE ADMISSION PRICES
CONSUMER PRICE INDEX
1935–39 = 100

		Adult M. P. Adm. Prices Index	Children's M. P. Adm. Prices Index	Combined M. P. Adm. Prices Index	Cost of Living Index	Retail Prices Index
1941	March	109.6	105.4	109.1	101.2	102.8
	June	110.5	105.4	109.9	104.6	106.6
	September	109.7	105.4	109.2	108.1	111.3
	December	111.3	112.2	111.5	110.5	116.7
1942	March	114.1	113.5	114.1	114.3	121.8
	June	116.2	114.1	116.0	116.4	124.8
	September	117.0	114.1	116.7	117.8	126.5
	December	118.9	114.8	118.5	120.4	129.7
1943	March	123.5	119.8	123.1	122.8	132.6
	June	126.8	121.4	126.1	124.8	135.0
	September	129.2	123.7	128.6	123.9	134.7
	December	130.7	124.4	130.1	124.4	135.5
1944	March	135.1	126.0	134.1	123.8	135.1
	June	151.7	151.7	151.7	125.4	137.5
	September	152.2	152.0	152.2	126.5	138.9
	December	152.2	152.3	152.2	127.0	139.6
1945	March	152.6	152.3	152.6	126.8	139.6
	June	152.9	154.6	153.1	129.0	142.1
	September	153.5	154.3	153.6	128.9	142.0
	December	153.5	154.3	153.6	129.9	143.1
1946	March	156.2	154.6	156.0	130.2	143.7
	June	156.7	155.9	156.7	133.3	147.7
	September	159.2	157.9	159.1	145.9	164.3
	December	164.0	161.2	163.7	153.3	172.7
1947	March	165.7	162.5	165.4	156.3	177.2
	June	164.1	158.5	163.5	157.1	178.7
	September	164.1	....	....	163.8	184.9
	December	167.5	161.0	166.9	167.0	188.4
1948	March	167.7	160.0	166.8	166.9	188.6
	June	166.4	159.4	165.4	171.7	193.5
	September	167.1	157.3	165.7	174.5	196.3
	December	171.0	162.8	169.9	171.4	192.5
1949	March	172.7	166.5	171.8	169.5	189.4
	June	171.9	156.1	169.8	169.6	188.3
	September	174.3	157.0	171.9	169.6	187.2

Examination of Table 66 reveals an upward trend in admission prices since 1941, although a definite leveling off of the index is noticeable beginning in 1944. Using the 1935–39 years as a base of 100.0, the index jumps from 109.1 in March, 1941, to 171.9 in September, 1949. Children's admission increased from 105.4 in March, 1941, to 157.0 in September, 1949.

To demonstrate how the admission price indexes correlate with the price structure of the U. S. economy in general, Table 66 shows also the cost of living and retail price indexes.

While the evidence in the table indicates that motion picture audiences were required to pay more for a theater ticket in 1946 than in 1941, any appraisal of the extent and nature of this increase must take into account the following factors:

The index includes federal, state, and local admission taxes (including general sales taxes). Consequently, fluctuations in the index represent changes in tax scales as well as variations in the net prices charged. The significance of this point is clearly evident in the figures for the spring of 1944, when the index jumped from 134.1 in March to 151.6 in April. Effective April 1, 1944, the Revenue Act of 1943 provided for an increase in the admission tax from one cent for each ten cents or fraction thereof, to one cent for each five cents or major fraction thereof.

Although Saturday, Sunday, and holiday data are omitted, the extent to which higher prices (if any) for these days is offset by lower weekday matinee prices (also omitted) is not known. In other words, these omissions may affect the index, but the direction and degree have not been measured.

Because of longer working hours during the war years, some industry observers are of the opinion that attendance lessened during the matinee performances but increased over weekends and holidays. Consequently, it is claimed, there may have been a greater tendency to raise prices for weekend and holiday performances. Matinee prices, on the other hand, tended to increase more slowly, if at all, and such changes may have been effected later than the weekend and holiday boosts.

No detailed explanation has been given of the procedure followed by the Bureau in computing the index. While the data may be accepted outwardly as representative of general price changes, it would be interesting to know the components of the index factor, the weights assigned to first-run against second-run houses, single-feature against double-feature houses, etc.

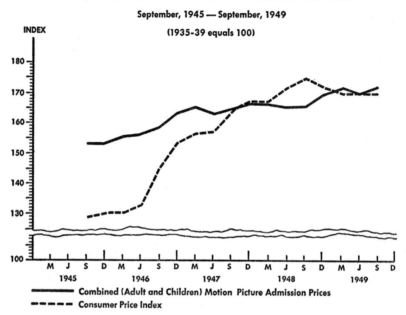

MOTION PICTURE ADMISSION PRICES AND CONSUMER PRICE INDEX

September, 1945 — September, 1949

(1935-39 equals 100)

———— Combined (Adult and Children) Motion Picture Admission Prices
— — — — Consumer Price Index

Source: U. S. Bureau of Labor Statistics

CHART 9

Chart 9 presents a graphic comparison between two index series, namely the combined (adults and children) admission price index and the consumer price index. According to the figures of the Bureau of Labor Statistics, the average increase in movie admission prices from September, 1945, to June, 1949, is less than one third of the rise in the general cost of living. These figures show the increase by percentages: consumer price index, 31.6; food, 46.6; apparel, 28.4; rent, 11.4; motion picture admissions, 10.5.

Only a small segment of the moviegoing public seems to feel

that admission prices are too high, according to a survey conducted by the Opinion Research Corporation for Controller-
ship Foundation, Inc.[3] A breakdown of statements of 875 respondents who felt that some industries or companies probably
make too much profit shows the motion picture industry in a
rather favorable position, as demonstrated by the following
figures:

Companies or industries making too much profit	Per cent of 875 respondents [1]
Food; textile industries	29
Auto	25
Steel	16
Public utilities	8
All business, large business	8
Gas and oil companies	8
Shipbuilding	7
Chemicals, medicine	7
All store trades	6
Electric appliance companies	6
MOTION PICTURES	4
War industries	4
Railroads	3
Insurance companies; real estate	2
Construction	1
Coal companies	1
Transportation (other than railroads)	1
Banks	1
Miscellaneous	7
Don't know	6

[1] Percentages add to more than 100 because of multiple answers.

It should be borne in mind that the above figures represent
opinions and not necessarily facts. Lines of business such as
food, which are hitting close to home, are therefore singled out
for frequent critical mentions. The relatively low proportion
of persons considering motion pictures as an industry making
too much profit is significant, due to the frequent purchases of
admissions by the average families.

[3] *The Public's Acceptance of the Facts and Figures of Business Accounting*
(Princeton, N. J.: Princeton University Press, 1947).

CHAPTER 14 *Film audience research in foreign countries*

While the motion picture industry as a whole was slow in recognizing the possibilities of audience research for its national market, the foreign departments of some major firms, anxious to expand the market abroad, have shown considerable interest in this approach. But motion picture audience studies in foreign countries are still somewhat sporadic, and our information about foreign moviegoing habits remains sparse.

The main difficulty facing a research director who is entrusted with an assignment to be conducted outside the United States is to locate the proper field personnel. Research workers are now available in almost every community in the United States where market and public opinion research has reached its widest usage; but for most countries abroad the questionnaire approach is quite new, and the necessary personnel and facilities are in some cases not available and in other cases not seasoned enough to be entrusted with important studies. The recent expansion of research into foreign countries, especially Latin America, is improving this situation rapidly.

Besides the selection of a reliable field staff there are other important problems. The translation of the questionnaire has to be done very carefully. It should be done by a reliable person actually living in the territory where the field work will be conducted. There are, for example, slight differences in the everyday Spanish spoken in the various South American countries. A literal translation may be proper for one territory and may be considered somewhat stilted in another. The questionnaire should be tested to make absolutely sure that the questions convey their meaning correctly. The sample also may present difficulties. The situation differs from country to country. Figures are available in some instances and are not in others. Considerable difficulty is sometimes found in establishing income group breakdowns, as the distribution of wealth in most foreign countries differs greatly from conditions prevailing in the United States.

When reliable personnel is available, it has usually proved advisable to conduct the tabulation in the foreign country under analysis. This is especially important when the questionnaire contains many open-ended questions, for it has been found that even foreign-speaking persons in the United States have great difficulty in reading foreign handwritings and in understanding the local idioms which usually show up in a number of the questionnaires. Last but not least, it is further important to have a reliable and capable research director or field supervisor in charge of the assignment who is familiar with all local problems. This does not by any means exhaust the problems of foreign surveys. It is merely intended to indicate some of the major considerations involved in these assignments.

As far as motion picture surveys are concerned, it is possible to designate two types of foreign studies which have been carried on with some frequency. There are, first of all, studies of a general nature which have the purpose of determining the composition of the motion picture audience abroad. These studies usually follow the same principle as similar surveys conducted for the American audience. Their main objective is to find out who goes to the movies and why, and who does not go to the movies and why.

More typical, however, are those studies resulting from the

language aspect of pictures distributed in countries where English is not spoken or is understood by only a limited section of the audience.

Pictures which are exported to non-English-speaking countries must be adapted for foreign consumption. Two methods are widely used. The most common one is the use of subtitles in the foreign language. For this purpose the prints with English dialogue are used, and a partial translation of the actual English dialogue is superimposed. This is a relatively inexpensive way of overcoming the language difficulty.

The second method is the synchronization or dubbing-in of foreign dialogue. For this purpose a special script must be written. The picture is rolled off again and a new soundtrack is made with native actors replacing the spoken parts in their respective languages, attempting as far as possible to follow the mouth movements of the original film. Segments of the original soundtrack which carry sound effects other than the spoken word need not be replaced. This method is much more expensive than the superimposing of subtitles.

A third method, called "narration," has recently been introduced by one of the major producing companies. In this case a new soundtrack is also recorded with a speaker explaining the happenings and telling the story as it evolves on the screen. The narration method is especially keyed for smaller foreign language markets and territories which have a large percentage of illiteracy, such as the Far East where a multitude of dialects prevails and where comparatively few people can read or write. A synchronization would be too expensive for many of these small groups.

In certain Latin American countries the different techniques of adapting movies have become the subject of some dispute, carried out both by the industry and the public at large. Shortly after synchronizations were introduced in lieu of subtitles, considerable pressure was exerted to change back to subtitles. The main arguments of this "subtitle" faction were that moviegoers object to their favorite stars having a different voice everytime they see them, that synchronizations were not well done, and that many people use motion pictures as a convenient means of learning English. Motion picture people argued that these objections are made only by a minority who know English, and that the average man on the street who does not know the language would naturally prefer the synchronized picture which he can understand without difficulty.

To get a clearer picture of the actual situation, one motion picture company decided to conduct a research study on this problem. The survey was placed in a Latin American country where this argument was especially prevalent. The sponsor of the study does not wish to reveal the country where the study was conducted, but he has given permission to quote some of the results which have a bearing on the issue.

The first step was to find out how many people understood English.

TABLE 67

QUESTION: DO YOU UNDERSTAND ENGLISH?

	Total	High	*Income Groups* Middle	Low
Not at all	59%	22%	54%	79%
A little	29	42	33	18
Fairly well	8	26	8	2
Very well	4	10	5	1
Total	100%	100%	100%	100%

The key question of the survey was worded as follows:

If you see American pictures, do you prefer them with Spanish subtitles or dubbed-in Spanish dialogue?

TABLE 68

PREFERENCE FOR SPANISH SUBTITLES OR DUBBED-IN DIALOGUE

	Total	High	*Income groups* Middle	Low
Subtitles	61%	81%	63%	53%
Dubbed-in dialogue	33	14	30	42
No preference	6	5	7	5
Total	100%	100%	100%	100%

The figures show that 81 per cent of persons in "high" income groups favored the original English version with subtitles. However, also slightly more than half of the people questioned who were part of the "low" income group spoke in favor of subtitles. The answers to the question about the knowledge of English suggests that the reaction of the people was honest and that the prestige factor did not decisively influence the results.

Audience research was called upon in another case to help decide a question in connection with narrations. Even though a distributing company tried very carefully to select speakers who would speak the language of the people of the respective territories, it was reported that these narrators were not always easily understood, that their language was too sophisticated for their audiences. To test narrators, special questionnaires were drawn up and translated into other languages. Test runs of the narrations were arranged for, and a sample of average moviegoers was asked how the narration was understood, whether the words could be comprehended without difficulty, and whether or not the narrator talked too fast. The results of these surveys indicated a much greater lack of understanding than was anticipated by teachers, officials, and other persons on a higher educational level whose judgment was previously used for deciding the selection of narrators.

APPENDIX: *The principle of sampling*

Samples are used to save both time and money in the development of information. A complete census of a population may take too long to be useful. Regardless of time, the expense of a census is usually prohibitive.[1]

The basis for any measurement by the survey technique is the assumption that a distribution of replies obtained from a limited number of respondents is the same as would be obtained if the entire population were questioned. The assumption is valid only when the small segment resembles in various ways the entire population from which it is drawn.[2]

The principle of sampling the population or, in our case, the sampling of the moviegoing public, is basically the same as the sampling or testing done in other fields of activity. A physician who takes a blood test to find whether his patient suffers from anemia needs only a drop of blood. He knows that the red cell count and the amount of hemoglobin in the sample represents exactly the composition of the subject's blood. A buyer of tobacco does not have to inspect the entire lot offered to him. He can content himself with examining a few leaves and judge from their quality the value of the whole lot.

By the same token it is possible for the public opinion researcher to ascertain from his population sample how the entire population or "universe" it represents thinks about certain questions. The poll

[1] Committee on Marketing Research Techniques, "Design, Size, and Validation of Sample for Market Research," *The Journal of Marketing*, January, 1946.
[2] Blankenship, Albert B., *Consumer and Public Opinion Research*, p. 98.

sample can be considered a miniature of the national population; if it is constructed for a motion picture survey it can be considered a small-scale reproduction of the moviegoing public.

There is, however, one outstanding difference between the doctor who takes a blood test, the tobacco buyer who examines tobacco leaves, and the researcher who tests public opinion. The physician can take any tiny drop of blood from the patient's body for his laboratory test because every such drop is practically identical to every other in the patient's blood stream. But the research investigator cannot approach indiscriminately any group of people for his investigation; for this group may be atypical of the population. Obviously a thousand twelve-year-old boys feel different on most topics than a thousand elderly ladies.

So the opinion researcher has the task of constructing a sample so that all the various population groups will be included in the proper proportion. If 5 per cent of the people in the total group under investigation are twelve-year-old boys, 5 per cent of this sample must also consist of this group. To scale down all the elements and characteristics of the population and obtain a perfectly comparable miniature sample would obviously be too difficult a task. Furthermore, special considerations require that the sample be set up in terms which will make it possible for the interviewer to select the proper types of respondents without too much difficulty. In the construction of nationwide poll samples, consequently, the standard practice is to "stratify" according to a few important characteristics.[3]

The product of this process is called the controlled or stratified sample. It is used by all reliable institutes and, depending upon the problem in various research studies, the sample control is more or less intensive.

The most common controls are those concerned with the distribution of sex, age, socio-economic groups, color, nationalities, and educational levels. Geographical controls such as the distribution of the interviews among different regions, in towns of different size, and the proportion of rural and urban respondents, are also regularly employed. The sample for film research studies is usually stratified in an additional way. The respondents are divided into moviegoers and non-moviegoers, and frequently non-moviegoers are eliminated altogether.

[3] Cantril, Hadley, *Gauging Public Opinion* (Princeton, N. J.: Princeton University Press, 1946).

The accuracy and validity of the results of research studies depends mainly on the following three criteria: the approach used for the problem under investigation, the design of the sample, and the size of the sample.

The approach to the problem in question is reflected in the technique decided on by the researcher in charge of the assignment. He had to translate and reduce the problem or the subject of the inquiry into simple questions. "Leading questions" which may influence the answers have to be avoided. The questionnaire has to be easy to follow by the staff in the field, and the questions have to be phrased in such a way that the uneducated section of the sample will have no difficulty in answering them. Also, the questionnaire has to be constructed so that the tabulation following the field work can be executed efficiently. This is of special importance when precoded or semi-coded questionnaires are in use, designed for machine tabulation.

The main statistical problem of the sample design is the formation of strata and cross-strata, resulting in cells into which the population will be divided. Need for a sample design based on stratification originates in the before-mentioned fact that social populations to be sampled are complex and not homogenous. The particular social elements which enter into the design of the sample are determined by the nature of the problem at hand.[4] For some studies, for instance, sex may not be an important factor since men and women have been found to think alike on the particular matter. In such a case it would not be important to stratify by sex, whereas it might be very important to stratify by age.

The responsibility for the obtaining of the predetermined sample rests partly upon the research management and partly on the interrogator in the field. The research management has the task of selecting the areas where the interviews have to be conducted, and in this way controls the geographical sampling; it can also select certain areas and streets in some locations where it is known that certain income groups prevail—and thus control the socio-economical aspect of the sample. Most of the other stratifications, however, are the responsibility of the interviewer in the field. It is he who obtains a quota of sex, age, educational, and other groups according to the instructions he has received; and it is his skill which is of prime importance to the outcome of any research study.

[4] Committee on Marketing Research Techniques, *op. cit.*

TABLE 69

ACCURACY OBTAINED WITH VARIOUS SAMPLE
SIZES AND PERCENTAGES

Size of Sample	Expected or Observed Per Cent				
	10% or 90%	20% or 80%	30% or 70%	40% or 60%	50%
100	6.00	8.00	9.16	9.80	10.00
200	4.24	5.66	6.48	6.92	7.08
300	3.46	4.62	5.30	5.66	5.78
400	3.00	4.00	4.58	4.90	5.00
500	2.68	3.58	4.10	4.38	4.48
750	2.20	2.92	3.34	3.58	3.66
1,000	1.90	2.52	2.90	3.10	3.16
1,500	1.54	2.06	2.36	2.52	2.58
2,000	1.34	1.78	2.04	2.20	2.24
2,500	1.20	1.60	1.84	1.96	2.00
3,000	1.10	1.46	1.68	1.78	1.82
4,000	.94	1.26	1.44	1.54	1.58
5,000	.84	1.14	1.30	1.38	1.42
6,000	.78	1.04	1.18	1.26	1.30
7,000	.72	.96	1.10	1.18	1.20
8,000	.68	.90	1.02	1.10	1.12
9,000	.64	.84	.96	1.04	1.06
10,000	.60	.80	.92	.98	1.00

Accuracy of returns is directly proportionate to the square root of the size of the sample, and increases as the proportion of replies within a category moves away from 50 per cent.[5] Here is this rule expressed in figures:

	Size of sample	Proportion of persons who know about picture X	Results accurate within [1]
	400	20%	4%
	1600	20	2
Or			
	400	10	3
	400	50	5

[1] Obtained accuracy expressed in two standard errors.

The size of the sample in addition to the proportion of the reactions finally obtained or estimated makes it possible to determine its purely statistical accuracy. It must be borne in mind, however, that the sample size has no effect in reducing any bias present. If too many members of a particular population group are present in the sample, adding more individuals will not help. Only when the sample is representative of its universe does the addition of respondents reduce the mathematical chance of error.

[5] Blankenship, Albert B., *op. cit.*

Table 69 computed by Albert B. Blankenship from H. C. Link's article, "How many interviews are necessary for results of a certain accuracy?" [6] indicates the degree of statistical reliability depending on the size of sample and proportion of answers within a certain category. The table is based on two standard errors which are, statistically speaking, a probability of 95 per cent. This means that the range of error indicated on the table is correct in 95 cases out of 100.

[6] *Journal of Applied Psychology,* 21 (1937), 1–17.

PUBLICATIONS *on film audience research and related fields.*

Adler, Mortimer J. *Art and Prudence: a Study in Practical Philosophy*. New York: Longmans, Green & Co., 1937.

Arnspiger, V. C. *Measuring the Effectiveness of Sound Pictures as Teaching Aids* (Columbia University, Contributions to Education, No. 565). New York: Teachers College, Columbia University, 1933.

Bell, Marjorie (ed.). *Redirecting the Delinquent*. New York: National Probation and Parole Association, 1948.

Bernstein Children's Film Questionnaire. London: Granada Theatres, 1947.

Bernstein Film Questionnaire. London: Granada Theatres, 1947.

Blumer, Herbert. *Movies and Conduct* (Motion Pictures and Youth: Payne Fund Studies). New York: Macmillan Co., 1933.

Blumer, Herbert, and Hauser, Philip M. *Movies, Delinquency, and Crime* (Motion Pictures and Youth: Payne Fund Studies). New York: Macmillan Co., 1933.

Box, Kathleen. *The Cinema and the Public*. An inquiry made in 1946 by the Social Survey into cinema-going habits and expenditure. London: Central Office of Information, 1947.

Brooker, Floyd E. *Training Films for Industry*. Final report on the War Training Program of the Division of Visual Aids for War Training. Washington, D. C.: U. S. Office of Education, 1946.

Buchanan, Andrew. *Film and the Future*. London: Allen & Unwin, 1945.

Buckle, Gerard Fort. *The Mind and the Film*. London: G. Routledge & Sons, 1926.

Chafee, Zechariah, Jr. *Government and Mass Communications*. 2 vols. A report from the Commission on Freedom of the Press. Chicago: University of Chicago Press, 1947.

Charters, W. W. *Motion Pictures and Youth: a Summary* (Motion Pictures and Youth: Payne Fund Studies). New York: Macmillan Co., 1933.

Children and the Cinema. Report of a conference organized by the British Film Institute and National Council of Women. London: British Film Institute, June, 1946. 31 pp.

Clinard, Marshall B. "Secondary Community Influences and Juvenile Delinquency," *Annals of the American Academy of Political and Social Science,* January, 1949, pp. 42–54.

Cressey, Paul G. "The Motion Picture Experience as Modified by Social Background and Personality," *American Sociological Review,* August, 1938, pp. 516–25.

Cressey, Paul G., and Thrasher, Frederick M. *Boys, Movies and City Streets* (Motion Pictures and Youth: Payne Fund Studies). New York: Macmillan Co., 1933.

Dale, Edgar. *The Content of Motion Pictures* (Motion Pictures and Youth: Payne Fund Studies). New York: Macmillan Co., 1933.

————. *Children's Attendance at Motion Pictures* (Motion Pictures and Youth: Payne Fund Studies). New York: Macmillan Co., 1933.

Doob, Leonard W. *Public Opinion and Propaganda*. New York: Henry Holt & Co., 1948.

Dysinger, Wendell S., and Ruckmick, Christian A. *The Emotional Responses of Children to the Motion Picture Situation* (Motion Pictures and Youth: Payne Fund Studies). New York: Macmillan Co., 1933.

Eichel, C. G. "An Experiment to Determine the Most Effective Method of Teaching Current History," *Journal of Experimental Education,* 1940, No. 9.

Fearing, Franklin. "Some Sources of Confusion," *Journal of Social Issues,* Summer, 1947, pp. 2–7.

Film Daily Year Book of Motion Pictures.

Film in National Life, The. Proceedings of a conference held in Exeter, April, 1943. London: British Film Institute.

Fiske, Marjorie, and Handel, Leo A. "Motion Picture Research:

Content and Audience Analysis," *The Journal of Marketing,* October, 1946.

————. "Motion Picture Research: Response Analysis," *ibid.,* January, 1947.

————. "New Techniques of Studying the Effectiveness of Films," *ibid.,* April, 1947.

Ford, Richard. *Children in the Cinema.* London: Allen & Unwin, 1939.

Forman, Henry J. *Our Movie Made Children.* New York: Macmillan Co., 1933.

"The People's Tastes in Movies, Books, Radio," *Fortune,* March, 1949, pp. 39–44.

Frank, Josette. "Chills and Thrills in Radio, Movies and Comics— Some Psychiatric Opinion," *Child Study,* Spring, 1948, pp. 42– 48.

————. *Comics, Radio, Movies—and Children.* New York: Public Affairs Committee, 1949. 32 pp.

Freeman, F. N. (ed.). *Visual Education: A Comparative Study of Motion Pictures and Other Methods of Instruction.* Chicago: University of Chicago Press, 1924.

Goodman, Ezra. "Are the Movies a Menace?" *Coronet,* July, 1948, pp. 35–50.

Handel, Leo A. "Radio, Movies, Publications Increase Each Others' Audience," *Printers' Ink,* July 19, 1946.

————. "Let a Hundred Million People Speak," *Hollywood Reporter,* 1942 Anniversary Edition.

————. "A Study to Determine the Drawing Power of Male and Female Stars upon Movie-Goers of Their Own Sex," *International Journal of Opinion and Attitude Research,* Summer, 1948, pp. 215–20.

————. "This Thing Called Audience Research." *Hollywood Reporter,* 1946 Anniversary Edition.

————. *Studies of the Motion Picture Audience.* New York: Motion Picture Research Bureau, 1942.

————. "The Social Obligations of Motion Pictures," *International Journal of Opinion and Attitude Research,* December, 1947.

————. "Research Laboratory of Tomorrow" in *After Business Hours.* New York: Funk & Wagnalls, 1949.

Hanser, J. E. "The Effect of Educational Motion Pictures upon the

Retention of Informational Learning," *Journal of Experimental Education*, 1933, No. 2.

Heisler, Florence. "A Comparison of the Movie and Non-Moviegoers of the Elementary School," *Journal of Educational Research*, March, 1948, pp. 541–46.

———. "A Comparison between those Elementary School Children Who Attend Moving Pictures, Read Comic Books and Listen to Serial Radio Programs to an Excess, with Those Who Indulge in these Activities Seldom or Not at All," *Journal of Educational Research*, November, 1948, pp. 182–90.

Henne, Frances (ed.). "Motion Pictures, Radio Programs and Youth" in *Youth, Communications and Libraries*. American Library Association, 1949.

Holaday, P. W., and Stoddard, George D. *Getting Ideas from the Movies* (Motion Pictures and Youth: Payne Fund Studies). New York: Macmillan Co., 1933.

Hollywood, U. S. A. Hollywood: *Hollywood Reporter*, 1948.

Hodgins, Eric. "A Round Table on the Movies," *Life*, June 27, 1949, pp. 90–110.

———. "What's with the Movies?" *Life*, May 16, 1949, pp. 97–106.

Hovland, Carl I., Lumsdaine, Arthur A., and Sheffield, Fred D. *Experiments on Mass Communications* (Studies in Social Psychology in World War II, Vol. 3). Princeton, N. J.: Princeton University Press, 1949.

Hulett, J. E., Jr. "Estimating the Net Effect of a Commercial Motion Picture upon the Trend of Local Public Opinion," *American Sociological Review*, April, 1949, pp. 263–75.

Inglis, Ruth A. *Freedom of the Movies*. A report on self-regulation from the Commission on Freedom of the Press. Chicago: University of Chicago Press, 1947.

Jephcott, Pearl. *Rising Twenty: Notes on Some Ordinary Girls*. London: Faber & Faber, 1948.

Johnston, Winifred. *Memo on the Movies: War Propaganda, 1914–1939*. Norman, Okla.; Cooperative Books, 1939. 68 pp.

Jones, Dorothy B. "Quantitative Analysis of Motion Picture Content," *Public Opinion Quarterly*, Fall, 1942, pp. 411–28.

Juvenile Delinquency. A symposium of opinion concerning causation through dramatized entertainment, expressed by noted psychiatrists, psychologists, educators, jurists, and criminal sociologists. New York: Motion Picture Association of America, September, 1948. 18 pp.

Knowlton, D. C., and Tilton, J. W. *Motion Pictures in History Teaching.* New Haven: Yale University Press, 1929.

Lacy, J. V. *The Relative Value of Motion Pictures as an Educational Agency* (Record No. 20). New York: Teachers College, Columbia University, November, 1919.

Lazarsfeld, Paul F. "Communication Research and the Social Psychologist" in *Current Trends in Social Psychology,* ed. Dennis. Pittsburgh: University of Pittsburgh Press, 1948.

———. "Audience Research in the Movie Field," *American Academy of Political and Social Science,* November, 1947.

Lazarsfeld, Paul F., and Stanton, Frank N. (eds.). *Radio Research, 1942–43.* New York: Duell, Sloan and Pearce, 1943.

Martin, Olga J. *Hollywood's Movie Commandments.* A handbook for motion picture writers and reviewers. New York: H. W. Wilson Co., 1937.

Mayer, J. P. *British Cinemas and Their Audiences* (Sociological Studies). London: Dennis & Dobson, 1948.

———. *Sociology of Films:* studies and documents. London, Faber & Faber, 1946.

Mercey, Arch A. "Social Uses of the Motion Picture" in *Communication and Social Action. Annals of the American Academy of Political and Social Science,* March, 1947.

Mitchell, Alice. *Children and Movies.* Chicago: University of Chicago Press, 1929.

Moley, Raymond. *Are We Movie Made?* New York: Macy-Masins, 1938.

"Motion Picture Industry," *Annals of the American Academy of Political and Social Science,* November, 1947.

Peters, Charles C. *Motion Pictures and Standards of Morality* (Motion Pictures and Youth: Payne Fund Studies). New York: Macmillan Co., 1933.

Peterson, Ruth C., and Thurstone, L. L. *Motion Pictures and the Social Attitudes of Children* (Motion Pictures and Youth: Payne Fund Studies). New York: Macmillan Co., 1933.

Renshaw, Samuel, Miller, Vernon L., and Marquis, Dorothy. *Children's Sleep* (Motion Pictures and Youth: Payne Fund Studies). New York: Macmillan Co., 1933.

Roethlisberger, F. J., and Dickson, W. F. *Management and the Worker*. Cambridge: Harvard University Press. 1938.

Rosenthal, S. P. *Changes in Socio-economic Attitudes* (Ph.D. thesis, Columbia University, *Archives of Psychology,* No. 166).

Rosten, Leo C. *Hollywood: the Movie Colony, the Movie Makers*. New York: Harcourt, Brace & Co., 1941.

Schramm, Wilbur (ed.). *Communications in Modern Society*. Urbana: University of Illinois Press, 1948.

Schmidt, George. *The Film: its Economic, Social and Artistic Problems*. London: Falcon Press, 1948.

Scott, W. J. *Reading, Film and Radio Tastes of High School Boys and Girls*. Wellington, N. Z.: Council for Educational Research, 1947.

Seldes, Gilbert. "How Dense Is the Mass?" *Atlantic Monthly,* November, 1948, pp. 23–27.

Shaw, Robert. "A Package Deal in Film Opinions," *Screen Writer,* March, 1947.

Sherif, Muzager, and Sargent, S. S. "Ego-Involvement and the Mass Media," *Journal of Social Issues,* Summer, 1947, pp. 8–16.

Shuttleworth, Frank K., and May, Mark A. *The Social Conduct and Attitudes of Movie Fans* (Motion Pictures and Youth: Payne Fund Studies). New York: Macmillan Co., 1933.

Slesinger, Donald. "The Film and Public Opinion" in *Print, Radio and Film in a Democracy,* ed. Douglas Waples. Chicago: University of Chicago Press, 1942.

Sterner, Alice P. *Radio, Motion Picture and Reading Interests: a Study of High School Pupils*. New York: Columbia University Press, 1947.

Sturmthal, Adolf, and Curtis, Alberta. "Program Analyzer Tests of Two Educational Films," in *Radio Research, 1942–43,* ed. Lazarsfeld and Stanton. New York: Duell, Sloan and Pearce, 1943.

Thorp, Margaret F. *America at the Movies*. New Haven: Yale University Press, 1939.

Tyler, Parker. *The Hollywood Hallucination*. New York: Creative Age Press, 1944.

——. *Magic and Myth of the Movies*. New York: Henry Holt & Co., 1947.

Wall, W. D., and Simson, W. A. "The Effects of Cinema Attendance on the Behavior of Adolescents as Seen by Their Contemporaries," *British Journal of Educational Psychology,* Vol. XIX (1949), Part I.

Weber, J. J. *Comparative Effectiveness of Some Visual Aids in Seventh Grade Instruction.* Chicago: Educational Screen, Inc., 1922.

Wiese, Mildred J., and Cole, Stewart G. "A Study of Children's Attitudes and the Influence of a Commercial Motion Picture," *Journal of Psychology,* January, 1946, pp. 151–71.

INDEX